Internet for Activists

Internet for Activists

❖

A hands-on guide to Internet tactics
field-tested in the fight against building
El Toro Airport

Leonard Kranser

Writers Club Press
San Jose New York Lincoln Shanghai

Internet for Activists
A hands-on guide to Internet tactics field-tested in the fight against building
El Toro Airport

Writers Club Press
an imprint of iUniverse, Inc.

For information address:
iUniverse, Inc.
5220 S. 16th St., Suite 200
Lincoln, NE 68512
www.iuniverse.com

ISBN: 0-595-23857-2

Printed in the United States of America

This book is dedicated to the Internet activists of the El Toro website team; John Berry, Dan Finch, Hanna Hill, Paul Hutchins, and John Santora whose unselfish efforts made a huge difference to our community.

It is also dedicated to the local officials, professionals, and other volunteers who served in our collective struggle.

This includes my wife Miriam, who, in a newspaper report, characterized the all-consuming El Toro airport battle as "a third person in our house."

Contents

Foreword

Len Kranser has written a book that should give fresh hope to even the most battle weary amongst us who toil as volunteers in the universe of grass roots political activism.

Written in layman's language, *Internet for Activists* is a how-to journal of the exploding potential of the Internet as a campaign tool that can be accessed by ordinary citizens to achieve goals of breathtaking scale.

The author draws on his considerable business acumen and combines it with his successful hands on campaign via a website to describe how activists defeated a well-financed steamroller bent on building a mega-sized international airport in their community.

This is a book for those who have put in years of service on behalf of various causes as well as for individuals who might want to get involved in public affairs for the first time. It should be required reading for every Political Science Major and a must read for anyone who would like to make a positive contribution in their own community.

You can't fight City Hall? Oh yeah, read *Internet for Activists*.

Tom Rogers, author—*Agents Orange; the Unabridged Political History of Orange County 1960-2000*

Former Chairman, Orange County Republican Central Committee

Chairman—Citizens against Unfair Taxation (1984), Citizens for Sensible Growth (1988), and No on Measure R Committee (1995).

Acknowledgements

Several highly professional newspaper journalists chronicled the events covered and wrote the articles used as examples in this book. It has been an education and pleasure to work with them. I particularly acknowledge Stephen Burgard, the award winning editorial writer for the Orange County edition of the Los Angeles Times who supplied the term that aptly describes what we were practicing these past several years; "a new kind of e-mail-based democratic activism."

As this guidebook neared completion, Mr. Burgard made the following observations about the project:

> The potential for the Internet to transform public policy debates in local communities has gone from being an abstract possibility to a reality. Just as e-mail and websites[1] were gaining popularity in the late 1990s, opponents of an airport proposal for a closed Marine base in Southern California took to their PC's. Len Kranser's explanation of how the battle over El Toro was waged is a how-to manual for activists interested in Web-based political activism. It explains how this battle was fought and won, and it suggests how the relationship between ordinary citizens and their government will never be quite the same again.

Stephen Burgard was recently appointed Director of the School of Journalism at Northeastern University

---

1. Mr. Burgard used the popular compound noun "website." Most writers use "the Web" and "Web site" as proper nouns. Except when quoting others, I use the less formal terms—web, website, and webpage.

Chronology of the War Over El Toro Airport

1993–Marine Corps Air Station El Toro, Orange County, California is placed on the Navy's base closure list.

1994–November—Orange County voters pass Measure A, designating the property for commercial aviation use in the County General Plan. The airport's size, cost, and impacts are yet to be determined.

1996–March—Anti-airport ballot Measure S fails in an attempt to overturn Measure A.

1996–August—County releases first environmental impact report recommending a 38 million annual passenger airport at El Toro and the closure of John Wayne Airport to commercial traffic.

1996–October—El Toro Airport website launches the first Internet site devoted to the reuse debate.

1998–March—The El Toro Reuse Planning Authority (ETRPA), a coalition of South County cities, presents the "Millennium Plan" to compete with the airport for public consideration. It calls for a mix of commercial, residential, and open space uses.

1998–March—County planners bow to political pressure and change proposed departure flight paths so that aircraft take off directly over mountains rather than impacting politically important North County cities. Commercial pilots object.

1998–April—County supervisors officially drop the unpopular idea of closing John Wayne Airport and propose to link the two airports with a "People Mover".

1998–August—County supervisors drop their high-density "Global Gateway" concept for El Toro in response to complaints over traffic generation. $4 million of planning work is scrapped. The County unveils a "Green Plan" for the airport to be surrounded by parks, picnic areas, and a golf course.

1999–March—The "People Mover" idea is scrapped as infeasible.

1999–June—A county organized two-day flight demonstration using rented commercial airliners backfires into a public relations nightmare when the noise raises residents' ire.

1999–July—The last Marines leave El Toro and the base is closed. A few civilian activities remain open such as a golf course, stables, a school, and a recreational vehicle storage lot.

1999–December—A new "community friendly" airport environmental impact report is released to the public. John Wayne and El Toro will both operate seven miles apart. Proposed flight paths are changed again, to bypass a North County city. The reported cost of the airport is doubled.

2000–The City of Irvine, which includes part of the base within its boundaries, steps up efforts to annex the entire property and proposes turning it into a "Great Park" to rival New York's Central Park or San Diego's Balboa Park.

2000–March—County voters pass Measure F by a 67.3 to 32.7 percent margin after thousands of volunteers collect a record setting 192,000 signatures on petitions to qualify the initiative for the ballot. Measure F requires that the County get approval from two-thirds of voters before constructing or expanding any commercial airport, toxic waste dump, or large jail within one-half mile of homes.

2000–December—A judge rules that Measure F unconstitutionally interferes with the authority of the Board of Supervisors. The initiative fails on subsequent judicial appeals.

2001–July—The county kicks off a $3 million "Just the Facts" public relations blitz for the airport with mailers to every residence, public forums, and a new website.

2001–October—The county approves a new environmental impact report for a 29 million annual passenger airport, but supervisors say they will build only two phases for 19 million passengers and 1.2 million tons of freight.

2002–March—Voters pass Measure W after it is placed on the ballot by another major petition drive. The new initiative is designed to accommodate the court's objections to Measure F. Measure W changes the County General Plan and designates the land to be used for park and education compatible purposes. Congressman Christopher Cox whose district includes El Toro and the Navy announce that the federal government will sell the land for non-aviation uses in accordance with Measure W.

2002–April—County Supervisors vote, 3-2, to support Irvine's annexation of the base for land use planning purposes and for Irvine to begin negotiations with the Navy regarding the disposal.

2002–July—Last ditch efforts are made to rescue El Toro airport. A new pro-airport initiative, intended to overturn Measure W, fails to collect the signatures needed to qualify for the November ballot. Newport Beach diehards and groups opposed to expansion of LAX continue to litigate and lobby for El Toro. However, most people believe the airport is dead.

Section I Introduction

1

A Tool for Activists

In the time period covered by this book, the Internet exploded onto the political scene. This tool dramatically changed the volume and velocity with which information is gathered and distributed to the voting public. Politics will never be the same again.

This is a how-to-do-it book about using the Internet written for grass roots activists. It is based on experience gained in the grueling fight over the proposed El Toro International airport, the largest land use battle in the history of one of the nation's most populous counties. However, it is written to help citizens win the thousands of smaller fights that erupt each year across the political landscape of our great democracy.

Cheryl Katz, a pollster for the Los Angeles Times, observed: "In a sense, the El Toro controversy and the ultimate success of people keeping [the airport] out of their area will serve as a guidebook for other areas facing similar battles. Orange County is the vanguard."

An eight-year war

On November 8, 1994, a generally uninformed public in Orange County, California, went to the polls and voted for what seemed like a good idea. They opted to convert the soon-to-close El Toro Marine Corps Air Station into an international airport. El Toro was to become one of the largest commercial airports in the nation.

Nearly eight years later, on March 5, 2002, residents reversed course and voted to kill the airport project. During the intervening period, proponents and opponents of the airport expended well over 100 million dollars and a million man-hours planning the airport, defending it, and defeating it.

In the same March 5, 2002 election, Cynthia Coad, the pro-airport chairwoman of the County Board of Supervisors, was turned out of office by the voters and replaced with anti-airport challenger Chris Norby.

The airport project was politically dead in Orange County.

What changed the voters' opinion? It was many things including the efforts of many people who gradually eroded public confidence in the viability of the airport project. However, both sides agree the Internet played a role far exceeding what was spent employing this new tool. Internet commandos, like military Special Forces, carried out tasks that could not be achieved by other means.

Growing respect for the role of the Internet

The rapidly emerging role of Internet activists in politics led the Los Angeles Times to publish a May 18, 1998 feature on the trend, headlined:

Invasion of the Gadflies Online

Bureaucrats beware; Public meeting junkies who love to air charges of malfeasance and sound off on issues such as El Toro are plugging in to a whole new audience.

The unflattering "gadfly" and "junkies" labels never appeared again. On March 11, 1999 near the turning point in the long airport struggle, the Orange County Register adopted a more positive tone:

El Toro Foes Get Savvy

Airport proponents admit that their opposition has become a formidable force.

...A webpage, complete with e-mail and hyperlinks...provides instantaneous communications to thousands.

Days after his 2002 election, Chris Norby, the new anti-airport county supervisor-elect sent this e-mail to me. "Thanks, Len. It all began because of your website."

Holly Veale, Chief of Staff to one of the anti-airport supervisors e-mailed, "Thank goodness for your website. That is really the only effective forum we have for getting information out to the people who care about the issue."

Jean Pasco, the LA Times' principal reporter on El Toro wrote, "You've GOT to write a book when this thing is over, Len." She added an emoticon (See glossary) e-mail smile :-D Then and there, I decided to write this book.

This is a case study about a volunteer-run website that dominated the web and e-mail part of the airport debate and impacted nearly every aspect of the campaign. It shows what dedicated citizens can do to beat city hall with this tool, hard work, clever tactics, and a miniscule budget. The book also examines other websites that entered the fight and gleans what can be discovered from their efforts.

This is a how-to-do-it book based on what we learned by trial and error as we went along. It is written for those who may need to wage similar local battles. It is a manual for grass roots Internet activists who are not computer experts.

From its launch in 1996 the El Toro Airport website developed into a principal source of information for journalists working at the more traditional media outlets. Because we dealt exclusively with one topic, our cadre of activists developed a better grasp of the subject than did many newspaper and TV reporters. Government and industry leaders access the website regularly to follow the conflict.

The website frustrated government bureaucrats by uncovering and disseminating public records that were never intended for the public's eye. Website requests for government documents, under the federal Freedom of Information Act and its state equivalent and their subsequent publication on the Internet provided grist for the daily newspapers.

Early on a pro-airport county public relations consultant wrote, "The El Toro Airport website is an almost limitless resource of anti-airport information." Janice Mittermeier, the County Chief Executive Officer, complained that the website "is actively and aggressively opposing current Board of Supervisors policy."

The Orange County Weekly labeled the website "devastatingly effective."

But most importantly, the website built a loyal following amongst the grass roots members of the campaign to stop the airport. Along with other websites that joined the fray, it provided the material for many hundreds of letters to the editors of newspapers and spawned thousands of messages to elected officials. With daily news updates and periodic e-mail blasts, the website team kept the public informed and involved.

The Internet played a key role in the final election battle to kill the airport at the polls in 2002. That election saw 2,000 volunteers collect 175,000 signatures on petitions to place anti-airport initiative Measure W on the ballot. Thousands of motivated private citizens contributed over $2 million for mail and television advertising to pass the ballot measure. The anti-airport websites were an important tool for communicating with this constituency.

Throughout the passionate campaign to kill the airport, the El Toro Info Site team of volunteers strove to maintain high standards of journalism. While the website's editorial policy was admittedly anti-airport, it provided access to both sides of the debate. The website's credibility grew as a result of presenting balanced news and issues coverage.

The Los Angeles Times praised the website with "People can see all sides of the issue and make an intelligent decision."

Thomas Rogers in his book *Agents Orange; an Unabridged Political History of Orange County, 1960-2000* calls the Info Site "An award winning website…attracting the interest of anti-airport groups throughout the world."

In 1999, the Public Relations Society of America honored the El Toro Airport website with an Award of Excellence for Internet and On-Line Marketing.

By March of 2002, when Measure W passed to end the airport zoning at El Toro, the website traffic had grown to over 500,000 hits per month.

On March 17, 2002, days after the election that killed the airport project, the Los Angeles Times editorialized that "residents with concerns about quality of life have mobilized and created a new kind of e-mail-based democratic activism."

This book is written for others who may wish to employ this new kind of activism in their own local campaigns.

2

Winning the War over El Toro Airport—a Case Study

This book is about the nuts and bolts of Internet tools. It is written as a case study with illustrations showing the use of these tools in the political war over El Toro Airport. It is not intended to be a complete history of the airport campaign.

However, if it ever seems to you that citizens can't fight city hall, a brief review of the El Toro controversy should provide encouragement.

Orange County

Orange County, California lies just south of the more heavily populated Los Angeles County from which it seceded in 1889.

Orange County is known as the home of Disneyland. The county is also known for having experienced the largest municipal bankruptcy in the nation's history in 1994, thanks to a risk-taking County Treasurer and poor oversight by the County Board of Supervisors.

The County is comprised of 34 cities. Airports, major parks, many public services, and overall land use planning are all centralized under the direction of a county government headed by an elected five member Board of Supervisors.

The state recently classified the population as approximately 55 percent white with the percentage steadily shrinking. The remainder is Hispanic, Asian-Pacific, and black in that order.

A plurality of the voters are registered Republicans. County politics tends to be dominated by the Republican Party elite and major land developers, many of whom reside in the wealthy city of Newport Beach. All five county supervisors are Republicans.

Orange County's population was 2,859,200 people in 2000. Charles Smith, a pro-airport county supervisor, was fond of saying, "The economy of Orange County is equal to that of Greece, Portugal, and Hong Kong. Can you imagine them without an international airport?"

Orange County uses Los Angeles International airport, LAX, in next-door LA County.

Orange County also has its own modern John Wayne Airport for domestic service. By some estimates it is operating at about half of its potential physical capacity.

Unfortunately, John Wayne is situated where planes take off over the expensive houses and boats of Newport Beach. Therein lies the genesis of the fight over El Toro.

As the battle progressed, the affluent and largely white Republican residents of the City of Newport Beach forged an alliance of convenience with the largely poor and middle-class minority Democrats living in the area near LAX. Their common goal is to limit growth of the existing airports that impact their lives and to build a new "NIMBY" (Not In My Back Yard) airport at El Toro.

The political line drawn on the map between the two counties allows parochial debate over whether Orange County is providing its "fair share" of Southern California's airport capacity. This "fair share" concept was propounded for the El Toro fight. It derives from a volatile mixture of airport, economic class, and racial politics leading to an argument for "environmental justice" in the locating of airports.

On December 27, 1999 the New York Times quoted one of Newport Beach's leading citizens in these words:

> George Argyros, one of the county's wealthiest developers and possibly the [El Toro] airport's most ardent supporter, cast the battle

in neo-Marxist terms. 'It's a classic case of class warfare to me,' Mr. Argyros said. 'The south county is all spanking new and they live behind their guarded gates. It's almost the working people of the north against the haves in the south.'

El Toro

For over 20 years the residents and City of Newport Beach have been looking for someplace else to move the jets.

In 1993, when the Department of Defense decided to close the El Toro Marine Corps Air Station, city leaders swung into action. They decided to convert El Toro, which is seven miles from John Wayne Airport and Newport Beach, to commercial aviation use.

El Toro proponents seemed not to care that the Marines said they were leaving because of limitations "due to air and ground encroachment around the airfield." It counted for little that El Toro is situated at the foot of mountains which jet fighters easily can climb over but which challenge commercial aircraft.

What mattered in Newport Beach was that El Toro was in someone else's back yard. It was in a growing residential area generally referred to as South County.

When El Toro was placed on the Navy's base closure list, the county and a group of South County city officials began studying aviation and non-aviation reuse alternatives for the 4,700-acre base. They had yet to reach a conclusion by 1994 when the pro-airport steamroller swung into action.

As many would eventually come to regret, members of the Newport Beach establishment skyjacked the planning process with a ballot initiative to designate the property for a commercial airport.

In California, voters can create laws through the initiative process. Petitioners need only craft a proper measure and gather the signatures of ten percent of the electorate to place an initiative onto the ballot. They then need a simple majority of the voters to enact it into law.

Two prominent business and political figures, George Argyros and Marion Knott, launched an airport initiative. Argyros is a billionaire and major Republican fundraiser. He recently was appointed by George W. Bush to be US Ambassador to Spain. Knott is a member of the family that founded Knott's Berry Farm, the county's second major tourist destination after Disneyland.

Their initiative, designated as Measure A, was qualified for the November 1994 ballot using paid signature gatherers. The campaign was conducted under the banner of Citizens for Jobs and the Economy, an Argyros-funded political action committee (PAC). The campaign promised jobs at a time when the local economy was experiencing a recession.

In 1994 no one knew what an El Toro airport would cost or what its environmental consequences would be. The first environmental impact report for the project would not be released until two years later. Nevertheless, Measure A passed by a slim margin of 51 to 49 percent.

For the next eight years the Measure A land use law would be the legal justification for county government to plan and promote an El Toro Airport project.

In March 1996 airport opponents in South County attempted to overturn Measure A with their own initiative, Measure S, but were seriously outspent and subsequently trounced by the Argyros campaign organization.

In August of 1996 the county finally released the initial environmental impact report, EIR, on the proposed airport. For the first time, citizens learned the scope of the El Toro plan. It called for a huge around-the-clock passenger and cargo airport at El Toro and closure of John Wayne airport. Opponents finally had a target to attack.

Anti-airport citizens and cities hotly challenged the environmental impact findings. Task forces formed to question every aspect of the report's validity. In accordance with state law, the pro-airport county and its consultants received, cataloged, and formally responded to thousands of submitted comments. Undeterred, the Board of Supervisors officially adopted the EIR in December at the conclusion of the mandated process.

The El Toro website

On October 21, 1996, at a grass roots organization's meeting during that environmental review period, Dan Finch an attendee stood up and proposed, "Maybe we should have a website."

At the end of the meeting I approached Finch. I said "If you know how to build a website, I'll fill it with content."

I was a recently retired businessman with a newly purchased home in South County and was looking for my next challenge. I'd been a school newspaper writer and yearbook editor in high school and college. It turned out that Finch was a graphic designer and had developed other websites.

Together we approached Bill Kogerman, Chairman of the organization. Kogerman reluctantly but wisely agreed to come on board with the idea even though we proposed to run the site for all of the anti-airport groups and not just his.

Within weeks, the El Toro Airport website (much later to be renamed the El Toro Info Site) went on line. The first article was a summary from the Orange County Register newspaper of October 15, 1996.

Pilots Wave off Easterly Departures from El Toro

The nation's 44,000 major-airline pilots will steadfastly oppose commercial flights at El Toro if the county insists on easterly takeoffs, because the pilots contend such takeoffs would be unsafe. The pilots' position, which conflicts with the County Reuse Plan, would put more planes over central and north county.

In what would become our hallmark style, we obtained a copy of the AirLine Pilots Association letter referenced by the newspaper. We typed it into a webpage and created a hyperlink from the news article to the letter so that viewer could read the full text.

At that time, several anti-airport grass roots groups competed for members and funds that they used to publish their own newsletters. Following the election defeats in 1994 and 1996, the often-fractious anti-airport leaders in South County recognized the need to cooperate if the airport was ever to be stopped. The movement's first unified platform took shape when the fledgling El Toro Airport website team undertook to Internet-publish the newsletters of all the rival anti-airport groups.

In 1997 an anti-airport coalition was formed. As website editor, I was invited to sit at the table along with the heads of the other groups. I later became the El Toro Coalition's second chairman.

All that transpired in the war over El Toro can fill a very thick book, but that is not the purpose of this book. The county government and over two-dozen cities on both sides of the airport debate spent well over a 100 million dollars on lawyers, consultants, lobbyists, and public relations firms. Private citizens contributed almost 10 million dollars to political campaigns that legally could not employ public money. The federal government incurred substantial expense. State legislators and Congressmen were drawn into the fray.

More than a dozen websites came on line after we launched our first one. Some were volunteer-operated, some were government-funded, and some were commercial. All of the other websites together probably never caught up in viewership to the original El Toro Airport website. Several gave up the ghost. What separated the successful sites from the unsuccessful ones is a subject for the final chapter of this book.

In terms of cost, the Internet was a miniscule part of the public relations battle over El Toro. This book explores why websites and e-mail nevertheless proved to be unique tools for marshalling public support.

The end game

Only two of the five county supervisors represented communities impacted by the proposed airport. The Board of Supervisors split 3-2 on nearly every vote regarding the project. The pro-airport majority arrogantly, wastefully, and ineptly steamrollered ahead with the airport plan.

On the anti-airport side the El Toro Reuse Planning Authority, a joint powers authority formed by the governments of ten South County cities, backed the fight to turn the tide with litigation, lobbying, and a powerful public information campaign.

The airport was doomed if only the citizenry could be rallied to take action. That was achieved through an alliance between the cities with most of the money and the grass roots groups with the manpower.

In 1999 thousands of volunteers led by volunteers took to the streets for the largest petition drive in county history. They organized under the banner of Citizens for Safe and Healthy Communities. The Internet was their pipeline of communication. For months dedicated residents sat at tables outside of markets, carried clipboards at community events, and collected a record number of signatures to force a new vote on El Toro. In March 2000 County voters passed the anti-airport initiative by a 67 to 33 percent margin.

Unfortunately, Measure F as it was designated was challenged in court and ruled to be unconstitutional.

The undeterred volunteers started all over again with a new initiative and a new petition drive.

On March 5, 2002, residents went back to the polls for the fourth and hopefully last countywide vote on the airport project. The new anti-airport initiative, Measure W, changed the county General Plan for the former base property from aviation use to a mix of park and educational compatible uses.

Voter turnout amongst the highly informed, motivated, and energized residents of South County was 50.9 percent. That was well above the countywide average of 41.5 percent. An overwhelming 87.3 percent of South County votes were cast for Measure W and thereby against the airport.

The next day, 6,375 viewers logged on to the El Toro Airport website to obtain the election returns before they appeared in the papers. Among the many who sent congratulatory e-mails were local residents vacationing in places as far off as Australia and Israel.

The Department of the Navy, which still owned the closed Marine base and ultimately controls its disposition, issued an immediate press release that they "will honor the will of the people" and dispose of the base for non-aviation uses.

The Navy e-mailed the press release to the El Toro Info Site for Internet publication.

El Toro airport was politically dead in Orange County.

Section II Building a Website

3

Hardware and Software

As the title *Internet for Activists* should imply, the use of this new tool involves a marriage between technical and political skills. This section deals with technical matters and particularly the basic hardware and software requirements for building a website.

To create and operate a website you need the following:

- A computer

- Basic software

- An Internet Service Provider (ISP) connecting your computer to the Internet

- A website host where the site will actually reside.

This chapter discusses the first three of these components of the system. It is likely that you already have most or all of the necessary ingredients. The chapter that follows covers the selection of a website hosting service, registering a website name and related issues.

The computer

Practically any computer built during the past several years will suffice. I began editing the El Toro Info Site on a 1996 vintage Pentium I with a 28.8 KBPS modem. It was fine for the job. Anything that you buy today will be faster. Currently, I use a Pentium III 420 MHz desktop machine with an external cable modem.

Most of us on the website team use PC's but one of our members uses a Mac.

A printer is a necessity in order to be able to make hard copies of some of the website information for use as handouts, speaking notes, and to preserve data that may no longer be on the site.

A scanner with optical character recognition software is useful for copying documents to the website.

Software

Building and running a website requires several types of software. You need the following:

- Word processor

- Webpage editor

- File transfer program

- Web browser

- E-mail program

- Accessories

Everyone on our website team has standardized on the same software so we can work interchangeably. This also facilitates training new website team members.

Word processor

Any word processing program probably will work. Some require tweaking of the preferences to avoid creating odd-looking ASCII strings of characters when it is intended to produce quotation marks, apostrophes, and the like. Actual formatting of the text such as selection of the type font, size, paragraph style, and so on is done in the webpage editor.

Our group's preferred word processor is Word for Windows. We use it to write and spellcheck the text of news, commentary, and issues material. Text prepared in the word processor is then copied into the webpage editor using the Windows copy and paste function.

Word also enables us to save documents directly in the webpage html format. This is useful when we receive documents for the site by e-mail and can use them without much additional editing. Much of the material sent to us from viewers, government, and industry sources arrives as Word attachments to e-mail.

Webpage editor

Our team's standard webpage editor is Netscape Composer, a component of Netscape 4.7. It is available as a free download from Netscape's website, so we have no problem requiring a new team member to get the program and install it on his or her computer. At one point, we tried upgrading to Netscape 6.0 but it was a disaster. We had incompatibility problems between machines running the older and the newer versions and went back to 4.7. If something works, don't change it just for some new features that may not be needed.

Netscape Composer may not be the most elegant webpage editor, but it works well for us. There are other popular programs. Microsoft's Front Page is available from some web-hosting firms and also can be purchased for a list price of around $169. Arachnophilia recently received a nice magazine review and can be downloaded at no cost from **www.arachnoid.com**. I have not tried it.

My advice is to use any popular program that you can get for free and stick with it. Our site may not be the prettiest, but we dazzle our audience with valuable information.

File transfer program (FTP)

An FTP program is necessary to upload your webpage from your computer to the website host's remote computer. This is done after it has been prepared in the webpage editor and saved on your hard drive. We use WS_FTP LE (Limited Edition) which is free of charge to noncommercial users from Ipswitch, the program's creator. Visit **http://www.ftpplanet.com** to download your copy. It is very easy to install and use.

The creation or modification of a typical webpage takes these steps:

1. Write the text in a word processor

2. Layout the page in a webpage editor and save it to the hard drive

3. Upload the page to the web host via FTP and the Internet

Web browser and e-mail program

Web browsers for viewing websites, and an e-mail program, come standard on most computers.

You can and should add additional browsers. I loaded Netscape, Internet Explorer (IE), and AOL software on my primary computer. It costs nothing to have all three. It's important to be able to see your website via these three popular browsers in order to know how it looks to various viewers. Pages that appear to be fine in one browser may be oddly spaced or have unattractive word wraps in another.

Some files that load in IE may not in Netscape. As will be discussed in a later chapter, some features such as credit card links for financial contributors may work in one browser but not in another.

Since we use Netscape Composer as our webpage editor, I use Netscape Navigator as my browser and Netscape Messenger as my everyday e-mail program.

Once our e-mail list grew to several hundred addresses, Netscape timed out and could not send the entire list in one batch. I then downloaded a free copy of Eudora Light, which can send several thousand messages in one batch. Visit **http://eudora.qualcomm.com** for your free copy. Operating e-mail lists is the subject of a later chapter.

Accessories

Clipmate is a non-essential but labor saving program that I have come to love. It is a shareware program available from Thornsoft Development for $25. To order it, visit **http://www.thornsoft.com**

Windows comes with an internal clipboard onto which users can copy one item at a time for pasting elsewhere, such as from the word process into the webpage editor. Clipmate provides an infinite clipboard. With this little accessory, you can copy a dozen or more items and then paste them, at your convenience, into one or more destination documents. Clipmate also allows the creation of multiple clipboards. For example, you can have one for temporary items, one for items of long lasting usefulness like addresses, one for names to add to the e-mail list when you get around to it, and heaven forbid, one for jokes to save and send to someone else someday.

Virus protection software is essential on your computer. We receive many e-mail messages each week with viruses in them. Most are not targeted at us but are forwarded unknowingly by viewers whose computers have been infected.

The first line of defense against viruses is restraint. I follow a hard and fast rule to never open an attachment from anyone I don't know. Sometimes it is tempting. I write back "We do not open attachments because of all of the virus risks. Please copy and paste your information into the message block".

But occasionally an associate we know gets infected and forwards a virus to all of us trusting souls. That's when virus protection software is a must. McAfee and Norton are two leading suppliers.

A **firewall** is important to those of us on the team with cable modems. The cable modem allows us to leave our computers on all day connected to the Internet. The firewall keeps snooping eyes from accessing our computer files. Zone Alarm is a PC Magazine favorite, is easy to install and it's available for free. Download it from **http:// www.zonelabs.com**

Optical character recognition software enables scanning of letters and reports into text files. The text then can be edited in a word processor. I use Caere's OmniPage Pro for Windows and find it very accurate.

The alternative of scanning pages of type into graphic files is not recommended. The resultant large files are slow to download and difficult to read.

Internet Service Provider (ISP)

An Internet Service Provider is the third essential for operating a website. The ISP connects your computer to the Internet for sending updates of your site to the website host via FTP and for World Wide Web browsing. Your ISP also enables you to send and receive e-mail.

Most ISP's will supply a web browser but you should add others as suggested above.

Some ISP's charge a service fee, and others are free, paying for themselves through the advertising that you and your mail recipients must view. You may not be able to run a website through some of the free ISP's. These services are only useful for e-mail and may not handle webpages or graphic files.

At the outset, I used Earthlink as my ISP. One of our website team members still uses their telephone dial up service. I switched to an always-on cable modem when the service became available in the neighborhood through my cable TV company. That prevents tying up a phone line all day. It's faster too, but connection speed is not really a great issue when building a website, because most of the work is done off line.

AOL is not my recommendation for creating or operating a website. AOL provides an integrated browser and e-mail program with its Internet service. It is very good for some users and some tasks but not for website construction and operation.

In emergencies, like when my cable company has an outage, I use my wife's laptop computer, which is connected to the Internet via AOL 5.0 and a phone line. I have not bothered to try later versions, but I don't expect them to be any better for the job. If you are serious about your website, you need to be serious about your ISP and use one that allows you to connect directly to the Internet when you log on.

Furthermore, AOL's mail software does not support hypertext links well. A hyperlink in e-mail specifically formatted for AOL subscribers looks like this when received by a non-AOL recipient:

> <A HREF="http://www.eltoroairport.org/">El Toro Airport Info Site—Index</A>

When formatted for Netscape, or Outlook Express, the link looks like this when received by users of those programs.

http://www.eltoroairport.org

Hypertext links in e-mails are important to our website operations. Viewers frequently send us information by e-mail, including website page addresses in the form of hyperlinks. Netscape Messenger and Outlook Express, which are used in connection with other ISP's, are more useful for handling this type of message.

If you build an e-mail list, you will need an e-mail program that is convenient for sending blind copies of messages. We always send bulk e-mails with the addressees hidden. That way we do not give away the addresses of our recipients. To send blind copies via AOL requires that each address be enclosed by parentheses.

We suggest that you ask users in your neighborhood for an ISP that gives reliable service. If you use a dialup service with connections by phone, select one that has a local number so that you do not run up telephone toll charges when you log on.

Website host

Selecting the service that will host your website on their computer is a big decision. That is the subject of the next chapter.

4

Naming and Hosting the Website

Every website is stored in physical form on a host computer configured to do that specific function. Large organizations like major companies or universities may host their own websites. Most of the rest of us use storage space on a shared server operated as a profit making business.

When viewers logs onto the El Toro Info Site, they don't access my computer in California. The request is forwarded, via the Internet network, to our remote host in Atlanta. The requested webpages go back over the Internet in response.

Whenever we update our webpages using the FTP software, the update goes over the Internet to the host computer where the new information is recorded electronically as an addition or replacement for what we had previously provided.

When one types **http://www.eltoroairport.org** (our site's domain name) it is automatically converted by the Internet to **http:// 64.226.131.145** (our IP address). The digits are our host's identification for our site. The conversion to an IP address is part of the host's service to its users.

On the World Wide Web it is common, though not necessary, to obtain and register a domain name with one service and to obtain hosting and an IP address from another. Once you have a domain name, you can move it, with some difficulty, from host to host. Let's start with the first step, which is obtaining a domain name.

Domain names

It would be chaotic if websites could choose any name they wanted without regard for whether someone else had already adopted it. Imagine a world in which you could select your own phone number without any restrictions. To avoid this the Internet has set up a registration mechanism to control the issuance of domain names.

Log onto Verisign Inc.'s website **http://www.netsol.com/cgi-bin/whois/whois**, and you will find a lookup service that tells which names are already registered and to whom. The site helps you to find other names that are available. Verisign Inc. is part of Network Solutions—one of the leading firms in this part of the business.

Dozens of other companies also provide website registration services for a fee. Use your favorite search engine to look for "website domain names", and you will find a large choice of offerings. They differ as to price and other services offered.

The other services, and particularly their hosting options, present you with important choices. But before discussing hosting services, there are a few additional comments that need to be made about names.

You may be able to obtain a free name and hosting through your ISP Internet Service Provider as part of their basic service package. Consider whether this will give you a name that is easy for your viewers to remember and enter from the keyboard.

> For example, Bill Mulcahy's popular Aviation Conspiracy Newsletter has the website address **http://pages.prodigy.net/rockaway/newsletter148.htm**

> For a while, the El Toro Info Site operated a free webpage with the address **http://ocnow.com/community/groups/eltoro_info/index.html**

I find these to be long and cumbersome to use. If your website is active and long lasting, you will be typing that name many, many times. I have typed or recited "**www.eltoroairport.org**" enough times over the past six years to consume days of my life. Recently, when .info addresses became available, we registered the shorter **www.el-toro.info** and linked it to our site.

When we began we purchased two addresses: **www.eltoroairport.org** and **www.eltoroairport.com**. They cost $70 each for two years. Even though the .org address was our correct one, about 10 percent of viewers went to the .com address out of habit. We automatically forwarded them to the correct address.

When the two-year registration ran out, I let the .com address expire in order to save the renewal fee. An opportunist immediately picked up the address and offered it for resale. We had created an audience and foolishly let it get away. The .com address was advertised for sale on the web for thousands of dollars. Fortunately our political opponents missed a chance to acquire the address, and a group that was friendly to our cause purchased it.

Today we see the registration of batches of addresses by one entity to protect the .com, .org, and .info variants of their website address. Multiple addresses can all be linked to one main website for a modest cost. We recently purchased two new .info addresses plus two years of linkage to our existing El Toro Info website for an introductory price of $45 each. We also purchased a .com address, abandoned by the county and a year of linkage for $47.

Names should be chosen with care. You will be referring to your website often, and the web address should reflect what you call yourself in press releases, letters to the editors of newspapers, and correspondence. Search engines will also pick up on the words. We began as **www.eltoroairport.org** and called ourselves the "El Toro Airport website". It worked well for over five years until the airport was killed, and we needed to adjust to a new reality.

Our website will continue as a source of information about the reuse of the former Marine base. That's why we acquired **www.el-toro.info** and now refer to the "El Toro Info Site."

The Peninsula Aircraft Noise/Safety Information Committee uses the acronym PANIC for their site at **http://www.palosverdes.com/panic/**. I wonder how well this works for them in keyword searches.

Website hosts

Your site and hundreds or thousands of others reside on the host's hard drives waiting for you to FTP updates and your viewers to log on by entering your web address.

Look for "website hosting" in a search engine. You should find over 100 offerings. Many are the same firms that offer website address registrations. Choose carefully, because once you start with a host, it can be challenging to change if you are dissatisfied. We know, because it happened to us.

You are totally dependent on the host's reliability. Research host ratings in publications such as PC Magazine. Consider the choice carefully. Reliability, pricing plans, and the services offered differ between companies.

Our initial host, located in New Jersey, turned into a nightmare. They experienced frequent equipment failures that shut us down. An operator once removed the hard drive that contained our site, and it couldn't be found for several days. We were told that it was "stolen" and then later that it was "misplaced". On another occasion their accidental switch of IP addresses sent all of our viewers to a Portuguese language website in Brazil.

The hosting firm eventually was merged into a larger company. The straw that broke our back and sent us looking for another host came when the new owners discontinued weekend tech support.

This was an important lesson. When we evaluated potential new hosts, we called their tech support in the middle of the night and on weekends and recorded how long it took to get through to a technician. Volunteers with day jobs may have to do some of their website chores on these off peak hours.

When checking out a host, ask about their backup provisions. We used one service that sent tapes home with an employee for safekeeping. He was away for over two weeks at Christmas when we needed the tape. On one or two occasions we found that backups of a corrupted file were also defective. Remember that making a backup does not guarantee that it will work.

Because we had added so many improvements and customized features to our site, we couldn't easily pick it up and move it. We did an extensive search for a replacement host. Our webmaster, John Santora, had to rewrite software and reconfigure a number of features to work with the new service. Ultimately, we made the switch over a weekend with a considerable expenditure of effort.

A later chapter will deal with accessory functions on a website. When evaluating hosts determine what software they provide or can accommodate, for searching your site, message boards, credit card processing, e-mail handling, and other features that you may wish to include. Will they provide multiple e-mail boxes and forwarding to you at your main and alternate locations like home, work, and a vacation address? Also determine how much storage capacity you will be allowed without extra charge.

Some hosts provide usage data that enables the website team to track the number of visitors, the pages they visit, and where they come from. Our site gets Webtrends statistics as part of the hosting package.

Interland out of Atlanta currently hosts our El Toro Info Site. See **http://www.interland.com/**. The company has been very cooperative. They provide online and real human tech support. On occasions when our site goes down for a brief outage, we can get fast believable answers about our status.

An all-inclusive starter package

A friend running for political office recently asked for advice regarding a campaign website, which would be needed for only a few months until the election. Many hosts offer economical packages. I steered her

to Verisign (**www.netsol.com**) as an example of what is available. For
$19.95 per month, or $129.00 for a year, they offer the following:

- Domain name registration

- Hosting of a 5-page website

- A matching e-mail address

- A library of professional designs that a beginner can use for creating
  a website

- Online site editing tools

5

Money and Manpower Requirements

It costs relatively little besides labor to operate a website like ours. The El Toro Info Site thrives on a few hundred dollars per year of expenses and literally over a thousand hours of volunteer time. Here are some cost figures.

Out of pocket costs

There is a cost to register a name and a cost to host a site. Registration of our primary **www.eltoroairport.org** domain name (URL) cost $70 for two years.

In 1999 we paid $70 to register **www.safeandhealthy.org** plus $25 for setup with our web host. We used that website for the initiative campaign to pass Measure F, the Safe and Healthy Communities Act.

In 2002 we added three additional domains that automatically forward viewers to our primary site. For the Measure W campaign we registered **www.yes-on-w.info** and linked it to **www.eltoroairport.org**.

After we won the election, we also acquired **www.el-toro.info** to make a point of eliminating the word "airport" from our lexicon. These two .info sites each cost $45 for two years of registration and the links to our main URL.

The County of Orange spent approximately $200,000 to create and operate a pro-airport website. In December 2001 the site was closed under a court order enjoining the expenditure of public funds to influence the outcome of the Measure W election. The county abandoned the **www.eltorofacts.com** website address and we registered it as our own for $35.

Competition is driving down prices. I recently saw an offer by Domain Name Registration for $15 dollars a year at **http://www. dotdnr.com/**. Shop around but be sure of what you are getting.

Our first hosting company, Digiweb, charged $25 for a one time setup fee and $25 a month thereafter. We received a monthly credit of $5 for putting their logo on the bottom of our homepage. Our current host, Interland, charged $406, paid in advance on my credit card for a favorable rate on two years of hosting service.

In our community, cable modem service costs $49 per month for the modem rental and unlimited usage. Each of the website team members has arranged for his or her own dial up or cable modem service. Of course, we'd have ISP service anyway so it's not really a cost attributable to the website.

As noted in a previous chapter, the software we use is almost entirely free or comes standard with the purchase of a computer.

It is difficult to measure but gathering information for the website adds a bit to my phone service and postage. We spend a small amount on handouts and office supplies. In total the website costs only a few hundred dollars per year.

Sources of money for the website

The team members pay everything for the website. It's our baby. We don't run banner ads, and our site looks better for it. If we needed substantial money, we would look for one friendly sponsor. If they insisted we would discreetly include the sponsoring firm or individual's name as is done on a Public Broadcasting Service television program.

Midway through our online life we ran one fundraiser by e-mail. We offered T-shirts emblazoned with our URL to anyone sending a $25 contribution to help "Kill an airport with a mouse".

The fund drive cost $49 to register a business name with the County in order to open a bank account and deposit the checks that poured in from viewers. We paid for the shirts after the money came. The fundraiser netted several thousand dollars, more than enough to operate the site for years. We donated the excess proceeds to the anti-airport political campaign committee and closed the bank account.

Some of the other websites that came on line after ours to take part in the El Toro debate were professionally built and operated. If you plan to spend $10,000 or more for a website, you probably don't need this book.

As of this writing, the El Toro Info Site is receiving 4-500,000 visits per year. Since we spend less than $4-500 a year on hosting, registrations, and office supplies, this works out to a cost of less than one tenth of a cent per visit.

In addition we deliver around 250,000 e-mail messages each year at no added cost. A local company, Dynamic Concepts Inc. donates their bulk e-mail service to help the cause.

Our principal website competitors each receive anywhere from a few thousand to less than 100,000 annual visits. Some are expensive operations. This is particularly true for the ones funded by governmental organizations. Their costs are estimated to run as high as one to two dollars per visit.

That makes delivery of some of their website messages more costly than sending an elaborate direct mail piece. It is important to analyze the likely cost per visit for any contemplated website project. One may be able to spend lavishly for a website that sells product and generates profits. It does not pay in grass roots politics.

Your website virtual team

Running a website can require a great deal of 24/7 labor. The amount depends on the amount of content and extent of the news coverage provided. The final chapter of this book will examine how several different El Toro-related websites approached these choices.

The El Toro Info Site began as a two-person operation. Our co-founder, Dan Finch, was the webmaster who knew the technical side of building the website. I was the website editor responsible for content. We learned enough together to be able to cover for each other when one of us was away. That seems like a good basic organization.

As this is being written, we have a five-member team. I still am the team leader and the editor responsible for content. It is pretty much a full time job. It includes a role as liaison with the other arms of the anti-airport movement and with the media. I operate as one of the official public spokespeople for the cause providing newspaper quotes and appearing on TV programs and at public meetings.

Dan Finch moved on and John Santora, our current webmaster, handles technical matters. Technical projects for the webmaster are vital though not as day-to-day as the work of gathering and publishing content. The webmaster's work comes in occasional big chunks. John had a lot to do when we changed hosts, installed our message board and added a credit card link.

A good webmaster will take the time to document the procedures that he establishes so others can follow them. John does this on a regular basis so I have a hard copy manual of the more technical aspects of the website's operation.

We added a team member, John Berry, to answer e-mail received from viewers and to send out targeted e-mailings. Two other teammates, Hanna Hill and Paul Hutchins, are reporters collecting stories from the print media early every morning and posting them to a section of our website devoted to this content.

A dozen or more other individuals, not formally on the team, contribute information to the website. Through their efforts we collect relevant news from close to twenty newspapers and magazines.

Our website viewership data shows that the busiest hour for the site is when viewers arrive at work and log on from their offices. My practice first thing after waking up each morning and before breakfast is to review the posts from team members, the incoming e-mail from viewers and reports from an aviation newsgroup. From this information I edit and post the top stories on our **Today's Headlines** page. We work as a team to have the news ready for earlier viewers.

The Orange County Register described this in a March 1, 2002 story, "In pajamas, Leonard Kranser goes to battle each day against the planned El Toro airport before seeing his orange juice or toothbrush."

Other individuals occasionally help to produce graphics, photos, and audio for the site.

As a virtual team we rarely see each other. We communicate mostly via e-mail. One of the members no longer lives in California and contributes regularly from the mid-west.

Motivation

Our operation has personnel problems just like any other volunteer organization. Egos get bruised. People quit because their ideas don't receive sufficient attention. We have lost good talent and gotten some back.

Long-term volunteer projects are fragile since participants are not tied to their roles by the imperative of a paycheck. "Burn out" is commonplace.

The team members are mostly inner-directed individuals receiving personal satisfaction from being part of something important. It helps that we are successful. The reward also comes from gaining recognition as a valuable force in the community. Our paychecks come in the form of occasional praise, such as this typical viewer's e-mail that recently was circulated to the team members:

> Thank you for all the support over the years…the blood and sweat has been appreciated…your site has been pivotal in the entire El Toro issue. Keeping it short…I thank you….My family thanks you…my community thanks you.

At one key point during the long battle, an anti-airport county supervisor hosted a party in honor of several dozen "Unsung Heroes" of the fight including all of the web team. It was a great thing to do for his political standing and for the honorees.

Activism is a people driven process. Success depends either upon your own individual hard work, which has physical limits, or upon your ability to attract volunteers to a team to carry on the fight along with you.

6

Publicizing your Website

We began with two viewers, my partner Dan Finch and me and zero visitors. The website now receives hits from over 15,000 different office and residential computers each month with many viewers logging on daily. On our busiest single day, 6,375 people visited the El Toro Info Site.

Other El Toro-related websites peaked after reaching only a few dozen viewers each day. Some of them have given up the ghost. This chapter deals with free and very low-cost techniques for informing potential viewers that you are out there on the web.

Other chapters will deal with assembling content that retains viewers after that initial contact and gets them to come back regularly.

Handout flyers at meetings

Inexpensive flyers can fit into a near-zero budget for advertising. Be there with handouts that publicize your website at gatherings of groups interested in your issue. To keep down the cost we buy 500 to 1000 flyers at a time at a chain office supply store that offers special low prices to unload unpopular colors of paper.

Since it's impossible to attend every meeting, publish your flyer on the website as a printable page. That way you can ask someone who is attending to download it and print a few to take to the event.

Get the website address included in organizations' newsletters

It was important to the development of the El Toro site to start Internet publishing the newsletters of the existing anti-airport organizations. When we started these groups had mailing lists of thousands of members. In return, they included our website address on their mastheads. Most of the groups are gone now, in part because the Internet is a faster and cheaper way to spread the word. Our website retains many of their former members.

Also publicize your website through organizations to which you belong but are not involved with the website's central issue. For example, I work with a volunteer group that helps small businesses. They publish news about their members' other civic activities in a monthly newsletter. I submitted a short article that included my website address and they printed it. Some of my wife's organizations also accepted small non-political articles with the website address.

Never pass up a chance to mention your website in your college alumni news or homeowners' association newsletter. Church or synagogue newsletters, social clubs, veteran's groups, or other organizations may print an article about a member's civic activities if it is framed properly and does not appear to be partisan material. We characterize our website as providing "news and research about the proposed airport issue" so that our anti-airport point of view is not initially obvious.

Respond to unrelated e-mail with your website address

You probably receive numerous bulk e-mails that pass along jokes, club news or political opinions. They are often addressed to long lists of recipients. These e-mail lists are gifts that can help you to publicize your website. The trick is to do it in a low-key way that does not look like spam.

Use the "Reply All" button, available in Netscape or Outlook Express, and send a message to everyone on the list. Send a blind copy so that what you are doing is not obvious. Brief replies might be something like this:

> Thanks for the joke. If you want to see another, log onto the El Toro Airport website **http://www.eltoroairport.org** and see the county's latest airport idea, or

> Thanks. Concerned citizens might also want to read El Toro news and issues, updated daily at **http://www.eltoroairport.org**.

Most of these replies will produce nothing, but it's a way to reach many individuals who read e-mail, and a few may be interested in your subject.

Reference the website in letters to the newspapers

Activists are prolific letter writers. Our website includes a page with hypertext links and embedded e-mail addresses for all of the county-wide and local newspapers in our area. We encourage our viewers to send e-mail Letters to the Editor.

When the news is the sort that may prompt letter writing, we include hypertext links to the newspapers within our website news stories. As a result we often see letters in the papers a few days later that originate with website viewers. The following are examples:

> The FAA report can be read online at eltoroairport.org and shows that the planned airport would delay traffic to John Wayne and Long Beach airports…or

> The Airport Site Consensus report, available on **www. eltoroairport.org**, eliminated El Toro as a likely airport location.

When writing my own letters, I try to include the website address. Some newspapers feel obliged to delete website addresses, as they do phone numbers, so bury the address as a reference in the middle of the letter where it has a greater chance of survival.

I frequently sign letters to the newspapers as Editor, El Toro Info Site along with our URL. That Internet address sometimes makes it into print.

Get mentioned in newspapers articles

The website started in October 1996. It received its first newspaper mention in the Orange County Register on December 12, 1996. It was our big day.

The County Board of Supervisors held an important hearing on the airport issue. I pressed one of our flyers onto a reporter who was interviewing attendees. His story came out with:

> Leonard Krasner (spelling my name wrong) butted in to talk about his World Wide Website, which is linking anti-airport activists here with those in Seattle and Chicago. **http://www. eltoroairport.org**.

The next day the OC Metro weekly magazine ran one of the letters I sent to every publication in town summarizing the airport debate and including our address. Ten days later the OC Weekly included a half sentence mention of our website in an article about one of the leaders of the anti-airport fight.

On January 31, 1997, a young reporter for one of the weekly community papers did the first full story on our website headlined, "Anti-airport web site gets 1,000 daily hits." We weren't quite up to 1,000 hits, but we were on a roll.

On March 17, 1997, we had gained enough attention, and made enough friends at the newspapers, to earn a front-page story in the Metro section of the Los Angeles Times along with a photo of me at my computer. We really were getting 1,000 hits a day before the story and that jumped to 1,600 in the days after the story ran.

Political web

Len Kranser is using a World Wide Web site to oppose the El Toro airport and believes cyberspace will be used more and more to drive home political views.

As the airport campaign went on, the website received more ink in the press. I became a spokesman for the anti-airport cause and have been interviewed on the radio and TV dozens of times since then.

For reasons that will be discussed in detail later, reporters for the major papers log on daily to check our news and to use the online library. I'm called regularly for information and am frequently quoted in their stories. As a result the website is well known, and the number of daily hits has increased correspondingly.

Building content that serves the traditional media and building relationships with the press will be the subjects of later chapters in this book.

Search engines

Search engines assist people who are looking for material they believe or suspect already exists. Searches locate authors, antique car parts, colleges, famous quotations, federal laws, and published articles. But, viewers do not use these engines to search for sites unless they expect the subjects to be out there on the World Wide Web

For the community website that means the public is unlikely to look for a website about opposing a new shopping mall, recalling the school board, saving a historic building or other public issues unless they already know from another source that the site exists. Awareness of the website must precede any search for its specific address.

Click on your favorite search engine and look for El Toro Airport, and you probably will find **www.eltoroairport.org** near the top of the list. The site ranks high with the search engines, because its pages receive a lot of visits, but the search engines contribute relatively little towards producing those visits.

In a typical month about 15 percent of the visits to the site are referrals from search engines. For the most part, they are visits that produce little benefit for the anti-airport activist cause.

Search engines probably yield most of the hits we get from over 40 countries each month. While some of these foreign visits are from anti-airport groups around the world or vacationing residents, we also get a healthy dose of hits from individuals interested in airports—any airport. Most of these visitors come to our site and stop at the homepage.

> I am a 14-year old boy who lives near Munich Germany, and I would appreciate receiving stickers and posters about your airport.

> I am planning to visit the United States in April and am looking to rent a single engine airplane...

Many visits come from Spanish speaking countries where El Toro is a popular search target. Asociación El Toro de Madrid operates a high volume website about bullfighting.

Our chief benefit from search engines comes when prospective viewers use one like a phone book. They know, perhaps from a newspaper article, that there is a website covering El Toro, but they don't have the address. The key point is they already know the site exists before they begin the search.

There are several ways to increase your website's visibility in the searches if you wish to do so. Website editing programs allow the incorporation of descriptive metatags and keywords in an invisible header attached to your pages. Some search engines look for these words when deciding what a website's content is about. You can list dozens of words that might appear in searches for your site. Our list includes:

MCAS, anti-airport, Great Park, central park, Measure W, Safe and Healthy, CSHC, initiative, El Toro, Lake Forest, Irvine, Newport Beach, Costa Mesa, Laguna, Leisure World, Dana Point, John Wayne, Orange County, O.C, Marine Base, Measure W, Agran, TRP, ETRPA, LRA, OCX, eltoro, SNA, LAX, Taxpayers for Responsible Planning, Millennium Plan, FAA, airport, Coad, flight, environment, CNEL, noise, traffic, pollution, reuse, eir, environmental impact report, Kranser, and others.

How much good it does is unclear. We know that use of these key-words produces unproductive e-mails such as the following:

Please help me to locate Corporal John Jones who was stationed with me at MCAS El Toro in 1972.

There are programs and services that can increase your search engine visibility for a price. If you are selling a product it helps to get the attention of prospective customers who are looking for your product and need to find a vendor. It pays to reach out to purchasing agents who explore the web for sources of supply.

With a public issues-oriented site it is a different story. Citizens are unlikely to go looking for a website that opposes condemnation of a historic building in the neighborhood unless they know such a site exists.

The activist does best to have his or her site listed and linked on other community websites.

Links

Links to related websites are a no-cost means to build traffic. We get about two percent of our visits through links to other public and private anti-airport websites. Early in our existence the percentage was greater. Today, we probably send more viewers to them than they do to us, but it builds relationships.

We link to all of our competitors' websites on both sides of the airport debate whether they link to us or not. It makes us look like the good guys.

We provide our viewers with a link to the pro-airport Orange County Business Council, a major force in this county. The OCBC refuses to reciprocally link back to us. They rejected our suggestion that they should present both sides of the debate. We argued unsuccessfully that it would help their members to make a fully informed judgement on the issue.

The county government initially refused to link to us from their website because we were opposing their position on the airport. A friendly member of the Board of Supervisors took up the matter on our behalf. The county finally relented. The results of this skirmish were several amusing newspaper reports on the controversy and more publicity for our website.

A pro-airport supervisor later protested the link because we were supporting his anti-airport challenger. The County Counsel settled the matter with an August 27, 1998 five-page opinion that "the links provided represent a genuine attempt to provide access to a full spectrum of views regarding the El Toro reuse issue, and constitute a fair and objective presentation of facts regarding the issue." The link to the El Toro Airport info Site is "a lawful expenditure of County funds."

Prowl message boards

We check Internet message boards that are apt to be read by prospective viewers of our website. Some are hosted by local newspapers, some by Internet portals, and some by other community groups in our geographic area of interest.

In some cases posters on these message boards include their e-mail address. We send them a simple single sentence message introducing our site. If posters do not supply their address, we put our message on the board.

Keep it brief to avoid appearing too pushy. Either people are interested, or they are not.

> For daily news updates, research reports, and opportunities for participate in the El Toro reuse debate, visit the volunteer-run El Toro Info Site at **http://www.eltoroairport.org**.

Paid advertising

It pays to advertise when selling a product that produces enough revenue to cover the cost. It doesn't pay to advertise an issues oriented website unless the money comes from a political campaign or public relations budget that is not intended to generate income.

We tried it once with a small ad in our local newspaper. Any result was so far below the radar screen that it didn't register.

During the political campaign to pass Measure W, the anti-airport initiative, we had a second opportunity to experiment. Thanks to $400 allocated for the purpose from the $2 million campaign budget, we purchased banner ads on the commercial website operated by the Orange County Register newspaper.

In the closing weeks of the campaign the Register editorial board came out recommending a "No" vote on Measure W. In a move that cheered our supporters and even amused the Register's editorial writer, we purchased 20,000 impressions for "Yes on W" banner ads on the paper's website. Many popped up on the online editorial page.

Our web traffic reports indicated that only around 4-500 visitors came to our site by clicking through the banner ads. It was not much to show for spending $400 but it was fun.

Political campaign literature

If yours is a website dealing with an issue that will be the subject of an election, include the website address in literature that is mailed to residents. Normally direct mail has a greater audience than anything the website can generate on its own. Some recipients of the mail may check your site for more details.

During the final election campaign to kill the airport, we were on the short end of a clever tactic by pro-airport groups. In California, as in many other jurisdictions, proponents and opponents have the opportunity to include statements in the official Voters Pamphlet produced by the government overseeing the election. These statements are limited in their number of words and are subject to challenge by opponents if they cross the line for legal standards for content.

Airport supporters who opposed our initiative included the address of their website in their ballot booklet statement. At taxpayer expense they were able to direct voters to website arguments made without limit as to their length or content. When the Voters Pamphlets arrived at each voter's residence, anyone who chose to type the address into their computer was treated to a healthy dose of misleading information that would have been challenged in court had it been included in the printed material.

By the time you read this, the campaign site may be gone, but if not, see **http://www.ocgreatpark.org/** for the "California Park Tax Assessment Guide". It includes a calculator and claims to show how much it would cost each resident in increased property taxes if El Toro became a park and educational zone instead of an airport.

The moral to the story is that it pays to be aggressive if you want the world to know your website exists. You will have to spend as much effort publicizing your site as you spend building it.

Section III Website Content

7

A Mission and Policies

An organization needs a mission. A mission statement spells out that purpose to viewers and to team members. It reminds us of why we are doing what we do. It also reminds us to stay on the path.

The El Toro Info Site's mission statement, posted on the website, is as follows:

This Web Site was established: (October 1996)

1. To facilitate communication between all persons and organizations with concerns regarding the construction of a major commercial airport at El Toro, California after the Marine Corps Air Station, El Toro closes in 1999.

2. To inform the public regarding El Toro reuse by disseminating information from the media, the government, the business community, local organizations, environmental research, and out-of-area groups opposed to airport expansion in residential communities.

3. To encourage citizen participation in activities which promote non-aviation reuse of the Marine Corps Air Station, El Toro site.

The second and third paragraphs of the mission statement make it clear which side we are on. The website's anti-airport editorial position is freely acknowledged.

Unlike some of the other websites that take a position on El Toro reuse, we publish content that is both favorable and unfavorable to our position. We do not give equal space to both sides but we are not one-sided. Coverage is balanced enough to result in occasional hate e-mail from casual visitors who perceive the site as having a pro-airport bias.

The site posts material from pro-airport officials and activists. The message board provides a sounding board for everyone. The **Links to Other Websites** page includes every El Toro related website regardless of its position on the debate.

Being open to "all persons and organizations" has enhanced our credibility and elevated the Info Site to the position of a respected source. Official government websites provide links to our site, government and industry officials take our calls, and media reporters consider our information to be factual.

Policies

Our first policy concerns privacy. We refuse to divulge our e-mail list even to other anti-airport groups. When viewers sign up for our e-mail bulletins we make it very clear:

> Addresses are kept strictly confidential. We never share our e-mail list!

We also have a policy on political endorsements. Local politicians seeking election in South County cities request anti-airport leaders' support for their candidacy. Some of these leaders give endorsements and allow their name to be used on the literature of South County candidates and on their fundraising mailings. I don't.

As the website received broad attention, I acquired community name recognition and was asked for my endorsement. Becoming involved in unrelated city and county political campaigns seems to me to be a digression from our primary mission. It could create hard feelings amongst our anti-airport allies running for office against each other. Consequentially, we added the following rather lengthy policy statement to the website. It is useful to have it there to ease the discomfort of turning down requests.

Policy on political endorsements:

The website editor and the website team receive requests for political endorsements and candidate recommendations.

We appreciate the efforts of the many candidates who have been involved in the anti-airport fight and the passage of Measures F and W. However, we will not endorse individual candidates, because they may be running against others who have also worked for our cause in important but less obvious ways. For example, it may be difficult to choose between an incumbent council member, who voted to fund [an] anti-airport budget or a city's get out the vote efforts at the expense of other local projects, and a hard working activist challenger.

We are a one-issue activity. We are unable to make an informed judgement as to the overall merits of each candidate in the many local elections. It is hard enough to do in our own towns. Frequently, there are contentious local issues about which we know little. An endorsement of a candidate implies an endorsement of their position on these issues over those of some other candidate.

We cannot rely on third party opinions or statements regarding candidates.

Therefore, we will do the following:

1. When asked by a candidate we know, we gladly will issue a statement regarding the candidate's activities on behalf of the anti-airport efforts. The candidate may use such statements in his or her campaign but this does not constitute an endorsement in the usual sense. We request that we not be listed as endorsing the candidate. We may give statements to one or more candidates in a race.

2. When asked about a candidate by others, we will indicate whether or not the candidate has to our knowledge been

actively opposed to El Toro airport. At the request of the Committee for Safe and Healthy Communities, we have published a page listing elected officials who have personally contributed to or raised funds for the anti-airport Measure W campaign.

3. In elections where the winning candidates can have some future effect on the El Toro reuse, we will actively promote anti-airport candidates who are running against those who are known to back an airport.

Importance of the mission statement

It's important to think through your mission and policies in support of that mission. It is too easy for grass roots activists to become so politicized in support of a cause that they lose credibility.

Victory comes from winning the hearts and minds of the majority of the public. Most of that public not only lacks your passion but also may find it intimidating.

Our Mission Statement is accessed via a link from the bottom of the homepage.

The page is shown here minus its unique black background, text colors, graphics, links and type style. Visit **http://www.eltoroairport.org** to see the real thing.

Homepage layout
http://www.eltoroairport.org

The El Toro Info Site
Internet Portal to News and Information on Reuse of MCAS El
Toro
Since 1996—100 % Volunteer funded and operated
No tax $$$$$ used for this website

Today's Headlines News Archive—since 1996 El Toro Litigation Yes on W Info Park initiative facts About the winning campaign	The next step Planning El Toro's non-aviation future. (Graphic)
Issues & Info Non-aviation reuse, Environmental impacts, pollution, flight paths, eco- nomics, property values, about other area airports Airport and park polls	Contribute Click for Online Secure Credit card link Help pay for the legal defense of W
Get Involved Meetings calendar Government officials' e-mail links	World-wide Links Pro- and anti-airport websites
Message Board	Search this website and the World Wide Web
Table of Contents	E-mail questions to the Web Team

About Us
The El Toro Info Site Virtual Team
Our Mission Statement

8

Organizing the Website

The El Toro Info Site is organized into four major areas of content:

- News

- Issues and Information

- Involvement Opportunities and Election Information

- Special features

When we began in 1996 we took inspiration from the long running Regional Commission on Airport Affairs website. RCAA is fighting a similar airport battle in the Seattle-Tacoma area. Visit their site at **http://www.rcaanews.org/** for a host of good ideas. Their homepage uses different terms, but they provide the same general areas of content.

After a bit of experimenting, we know we've got our division of content right, because the leading pro-El Toro airport website copied our format.

The homepage

The function of the website homepage is to guide viewers into these four areas and their principal subdivisions.

Increasingly, website designers are arranging homepages with tabs in a masthead across the top of the page and lists of links down the left side to facilitate searching. The Los Angeles Times website is an example of such a layout. See **http://www.latimes.com**

John Santora, our webmaster, recently developed such an arrangement for our site. For better or worse we did not go to the effort of implementing this major redesign. The decision was to put all of our energies into defeating the airport rather than perfecting the website.

Unfortunately, we did not save every change in our homepage appearance as it slowly evolved over the years. It would chronicle our development like a family photo album. Most of the early versions are lost, written over in a constant process of updating. Save your early homepages for nostalgic reasons and in case you write a book.

Our November 18, 2000 homepage is one of the oldest retained. It is preserved on the web at **http://www.eltoroairport.org/ index111800.html**. It makes the division into content areas particularly clear. It also includes an animated airplane graphic that was our symbol for several years.

News

Most viewers come to the website for news about El Toro. The **Message Board** comes second, and the **Issues Section** is third in popularity. A later section of this book will discuss newsgathering practices and why viewers rely so heavily on the website for news.

The starting place for anyone looking for news is the **Today's Headlines** link prominently located near the top of the homepage. It is hypertext linked to the Current News page.

When we began the Current News page covered three months. Then it was archived and a fresh page begun. As our coverage intensified, we were adding new reports daily and sometimes several times per day. To keep the Current News file small enough for fast downloading, we switched to archiving it and beginning a fresh page monthly.

Viewers clicking on **News Archive** directly below **Today's Headlines** are linked to a secondary homepage for the News Section. That page includes links to each month's archived news, back to 1996.

Our news section also includes a **Litigation** sub-section where we report the status of the large number of lawsuits generated by the El Toro conflict.

We include a link to **Media Commentary**, a library of our favorite newspaper editorials and political cartoons. The Los Angeles Times gave permission to reproduce theirs and other newspapers have not asserted their copyrights.

There is also a page of **Letters** that began with viewer comments before we had a message board but now is a depository for statements on our issue from elected officials.

In the RCAA website the News category includes Action Alerts and Press releases, which we incorporate into our latest news stories.

RCAA also publishes a newsletter online. We prefer to send out e-mail bulletins that are similar to a newsletter and fill them with content that is already in our website news. There is more on this in the chapters on e-mail.

Issues and Information

Most viewers come to our site for the news, but our most valuable contribution to the cause may be the section on **Issues and Info**. The RCAA website calls this their **Library**.

As with other main sections of the website, a secondary homepage lists the contents of the section. It is a unique library of documents, data, reports, and polls on El Toro reuse, economics and logistics, politics and public reaction, airport plans, aircraft noise, pollution studies, safety, regional aviation demand studies, and facts about other area airports.

We have posted the results of every published public opinion poll on El Toro.

Here is where you will find demographic data for the region, population growth projections, studies of passengers using the existing airports, and aviation industry comments on the El Toro project.

Our stories in the **News Section** often include hypertext links to **Issues** section articles as background for the news. Our viewers mine this wealth of data when writing letters to the newspapers. News reporters who regularly cover El Toro use the library as a resource. We frequently refer new reporters to documents in this section to help them to tell the story accurately.

If you are fighting for a cause that has factual basis, you should collect those facts in an online reference library.

Involvement opportunities

A grass roots cause needs citizen involvement. As noted earlier, our Mission Statement says we exist, "to encourage citizen participation…" Your website will need one or more sections to facilitate this activity.

In California citizens can enact laws by popular vote through the initiative process. Because the El Toro fight precipitated four countywide initiative campaigns, our involvement content is broken into two sections. One is the longstanding **Get Involved Section,** and the other is the **Elections Section,** which takes greater or lesser prominence during the political cycle.

A sub-homepage in the **Get Involved Section** leads viewers to the following: e-mail links to elected officials, e-mail links for sending letters to the editors of newspapers, a calendar of important community meetings, and contact information for groups involved in the issue.

We include a printable one-page flyer, The Case Against El Toro Airport, that viewers can download and take to meetings as a handout.

The section also includes guidance for homeowner associations, PTAs, and the clergy as to what others are doing and how they can participate in the cause. These players were slow to come to the fore in the airport fight but eventually became very active.

Homeowners associations contributed hundreds of thousands of dollars to protect residents' property values and quality of life once they were shown it is legal to do so. One leading clergyman was a key fundraiser, another offered his church for a large rally, and a third delighted meeting participants with his prayer, "May only angels fly over El Toro."

Elections

The **Elections Section**, a specialized form of involvement content, includes the text of voting material, official ballot arguments from both sides, and relevant reports.

A sub-section on campaign participation provides contact addresses for campaign area captains, directions to the campaign office, means to contribute to the cause, and a photo album of volunteers in action. Digital cameras have made it easy for viewers to e-mail photos for inclusion.

Special features

This is the catchall section for the website's whistles and bells. Several of these features will be discussed in a later section of this book. We provide a **Message Board**, an e-mail link for writing to the website team, a page of **Links** to other websites, a **Search** feature for our website and the entire World Wide Web, a **Table of Contents**, and during political campaigns, a link for credit card contribution.

We are cautious about adding special features that add to the home-page file size and speed of loading.

Let's turn now to lessons we learned about building content.

9

Building Content

Content creates viewership

For commercial websites, viewers are drawn back to the site over and over again by their continuing needs to arrange travel, or send greeting cards, or buy gifts. Issues-oriented sites are different. Constantly updated content is what draws viewers back to public affairs websites.

Some websites are static but the more successful ones are dynamic in terms of content.

The static ones that make infrequent changes sit there month after month like the faces on Mt. Rushmore waiting for their potential audience to come once and probably not return. That is not to say that the one visit may not be important. However, your site will not generate a lot of volume if your traffic is limited to a single visit from each concerned citizen in a small city, a school district, or any other local area.

Some of the dozen or so El Toro related websites that sprang up in Orange County initially received several dozen visits a day and then petered out. Such low volume sites continue until it comes time to write another check to renew the registration or hosting service. Then they are gone.

To maintain a dynamic site that draws viewers back again requires considerable effort. The content must be updated frequently. Creating content is the subject of this and the following chapters.

This is not about newspaper-type content like comic strips, stock market reports, or daily horoscopes. One of the pro-airport websites gives the daily weather report, but it is hard to see how this helps to promote El Toro airport. What is needed is good intelligence on the issue.

Knowledgeable and motivated viewers are the major product of an issues-oriented website. Well informed activists are the people who write the most persuasive letters to the newspapers, ask the best questions at public meetings, and dominate the call-in radio and TV shows. They are the opinion leaders who tell their friends, neighbors, and co-workers what to do about the issue at hand. They multiply the reach of the website message.

In a petition drive each activist collects hundreds of signatures. They distribute literature to their neighbors. They staff phone banks. All the while they are answering questions as to why they support the cause. Each activist influences hundreds or thousands of other people. They are the cadres that win the battle.

Gathering news content

When the El Toro Info Site started, it was totally dependent on Orange County newspapers and local anti-airport organization newsletters for content.

Today the website posts an average of around two news stories a day. Only half are from the papers. About one story a week comes from a media source outside of the county. Nearly half of what is posted on the site comes from our own reporting.

This expansion of content from sources other than the traditional press is one of the reasons why the website is considered by many to be the principal source of news about El Toro. It also explains why most of the area's news reporters covering the issue check out our site each morning.

Several members of the website team scan the newspapers and their websites for articles of interest. Paul Hutchins, a very early riser, and Hanna Hill, who now lives two time zones east of Orange County, gather the day's newspaper stories from the web before most of us are awake. They post these on the **Early Bird** thread of our **Message Board** that will be discussed in a later chapter.

Other viewers comprising a part of our unlimited virtual team chip in with articles from newspapers, wire services, and websites outside of the county. They post these to the message board or e-mail them to us. This expanded organization works for the most meager of wages—just an e-mail thanks, and the satisfaction of sometimes seeing their contribution appear in Today's Headlines. We depend on input from these alert viewers.

Our regular coverage includes the Los Angeles Times, Orange County Register, Newport Beach Daily Pilot, OC Weekly, OC Metro, and OC Business Journal. Viewers also pick up pieces from the several local weekly community papers, the Wall Street Journal, New York Times, USA Today, Los Angeles and San Diego County papers, our competitors' sites, and various news websites. It's a small world these days.

I also receive the Aviation Watch e-mail bulletins sent daily by anti-airport activists who submit from around the world via a Yahoo newsgroup. Your issues-oriented campaign might benefit from creating a newsgroup.

Some websites publish the full text of newspaper articles without going to the trouble of editing, condensing, or embellishing. We do it the hard way, editing every article for these reasons:

- It avoids copyright infringement

- A shorter format works better on the web

- We frequently add hypertext links to related news and issues articles

- Newspaper articles are often too simplified for our well-informed readers

- We correct reporters' errors of fact

- We add commentary

For in-depth coverage of important events we rely heavily on personally written reports from activist supporters. They attend the numerous county, city, and pro-airport group meetings. Before she moved away dedicated activist Hanna Hill began the practice by anticipating questions about "What happened last night?" She would sit through long meetings that often ran to midnight and then type out her views on what transpired. At first she e-mailed them to a few dozen of her closest group, but later we broadened the circle by providing her own page on the website.

Today, these first hand accounts of meetings originate from several activists. They arrive by e-mail and also appear on the message boards. Most migrate into the website news days before they appear—if they appear at all—in the newspapers.

The speed with which we report was apparent after the abrupt resignation of the head of a group seeking to qualify a so-called V-plan airport initiative for the November 2002 ballot. He e-mailed his resignation to the website. We posted a report on June 7, 2002 and the first newspaper story appeared five days later.

> El Toro Info Site Report, June 7, 2002
> **V-Plan promoter Niewiarowski quits**
>
> Daily Pilot, June 12, 2002
> **V-plan leader quits group**

As editor I write some of the website news reports either by sitting through County Board of Supervisors meetings or by listening to the meetings online via an audio link while doing other computer work. The latter method enables the website to post reports while the meetings are still in progress.

Last but not least, the El Toro Info Site, like any serious news organization, has developed good contacts with key individuals who call or send us material for news articles. Sometimes these fall into the category of "leaks".

For example, we posted a key PowerPoint presentation—prepared by county staff for presentation to the Board of Supervisors—for our viewers to see before it was shown to the supervisors. Thanks to e-mail we can publish PowerPoint and other presentation material from Washington before it is generally available in Orange County. It doesn't happen every day, but when such a coup does occur, it reinforces grass roots confidence that no one in the government is going to get away with anything anymore.

There is no place to hide. Every ill-turned phrase and false move is exposed to public scrutiny. The relentless spotlight on Orange County government operations from multiple directions played a part in the departure from office of a pro-airport County Executive Officer, all four El Toro development program heads, and the Chairwoman of the Board of Supervisors.

The next chapter of this book deals with the Freedom of Information Act and local "open government" laws. These enable citizens to access a wealth of government records. They are powerful information gathering tools if you live in a city, school district, or other jurisdiction subject to these laws.

Issues content

Our most visited page is the current news in **Today's Headlines.** In many ways our most useful pages are in the **Issues Section** where we store articles of lasting value in an online library. We learned to build this library from the website of the Regional Commission on Airport Affairs; a group that was fighting the expansion of Seattle-Tacoma Airport well before we ever began our fight. When we began in 1996 they had the best airport-related online library available anywhere.

We frequently link news stories to relevant issue pieces so as to increase viewer awareness of the wealth of information that can be brought to bear on the matter at hand. Consequently our site is "sticky", a good feature in website parlance. Viewers spend an average of about 8 minutes per visit.

Issue-related material is gathered in much the same way as other content. You may have to be a little more aggressive in reaching to outside organizations to obtain some of this information. Visit our website **Issues Section** for ideas as to the scope of what can be collected.

The following is a sampling of about one-quarter of the pages in the El Toro Info Site library. It illustrates the types of information that are available and the kinds of sources that can be tapped, summarized, posted, and used in a public education campaign.

> **Irvine's Plan**—The City responds quickly to the Navy's intent to sell base property in order to raise revenue. (Provided on diskette by the City Planning Department)
>
> **Early Survey Sketched a Non-Aviation Future**—Project 99 supporters rate 20 non-aviation reuses for the MCAS site. (From the newsletter of a grass roots organization, provided by e-mail).
>
> **Two-airport plan**—Digest of informed industry statements on why the county's two-airport plan for El Toro and John Wayne won't fly. (Collected from public records and letters from the website editor to airline officials.)
>
> **Website noise demo**—A computerized simulation of where the noise will be loudest. (Courtesy of another anti-airport website and modified by John Santora, our webmaster)
>
> **Aircraft Noise and Capacity Act of 1990**—Congress ruled out local curfews and restrictions for El Toro like those in effect at John Wayne airport. (Federal website search)
>
> **Effects of Aircraft Noise on Children**—A team of researchers, including UCI scientists, look at the impact on children near LAX. (Abstract from a technical journal by one of our team members. A popular handout at PTA and School Board meetings.)
>
> **Kids Near Airports Don't Read as Well.**—Experts at Cornell University report on their study of the impact of noise on children.

(Study was mentioned in Newsweek where it was spotted by a website reader. Cornell e-mailed the report at our request.)

Aircraft Noise and Blood Pressure—Study links aircraft noise and blood pressure. (Occupational and Environmental Medicine magazine, picked up by Reuters and then by one of our viewers)

Airport Health Risks—Reports on carcinogens in the air near the proposed El Toro and John Wayne airports. (Technical paper by employees at one of the county's consultants, presented at a technical society meeting and e-mailed to the website)

Boston Logan Airport study—A study by a Boston suburb, Winthrop, found that for the most common respiratory diseases, asthma, and allergies are twice as common in neighborhoods closest to the airport. (Circulated amongst anti-airport groups on the Aviation Watch newsgroup.)

FAA Airspace Analysis—El Toro flight paths proposed by the county can be safely operated but are not the best, will seriously impact regional airspace, and reduce overall efficiency. (From the FAA website)

AirLine Pilots Association—The union representing 55,000 pilots comments on El Toro and the EIR. ALPA says they will refuse to fly on runways as planned by the county. They also state that John Wayne will have to close, for safety reasons, if El Toro is built. Link to several other ALPA letters. (Letters provided by the Association)

Federal Aviation Administration Memo—An internal FAA memo says that there is not enough airspace for two airports...so why build El Toro? (Unearthed amongst documents delivered in response to a Freedom of Information Act request)

Loss of Property Value and Property Tax Revenue Attributable to El Toro Airport Noise—A 2002 study of the loss in value and tax revenue in Orange County. (Prepared by a candidate for the office of County Auditor)

The Impacts of an Airport on Property Values—Editorial looks at the logic and data on how airports impact property values. An FAA study and Washington State study are referenced. (Summarized from the RCAA online library)

The Impact of Airport Noise on Residential Real Estate—Randall Bell, a nationally recognized expert in real estate and environmental damage valuation takes an updated look at the subject. (Copy of his study provided as e-mail by the author)

Avigation Easements—Homeowners may be required to give up their right to sue for aircraft related damages. (Written by a local attorney and activist)

LAX Demand Study—Los Angeles 2/28/00 study sheds light on limited future demand for airports in Orange County. (Summarized from a report prepared by Los Angeles World Airports)

Population Trends—Southern California Association of Governments projects the population for the counties of Southern California. Orange County is the slowest grower. See also that greater growth is in the North vs. South County. (Summarized data from Southern California Association of Governments and U.S. Census reports)

John Wayne airport photos—See why the County advertises the airport as "crowd free". (A photo essay with digitally provided photos taken by a local activist)

John Wayne Airport Utilization—Passenger, flight and cargo statistics for the airport from 1996 to present. (Running compilation of data collected from the airport's website)

Poll on JWA Caps—An e-mail poll of website viewers finds strong opposition to extending the JWA caps until 2025. (El Toro Info Site poll results)

Airport Site Consensus—1990 report recommends March, Pendleton and two other sites and rejects El Toro. (Summary by an activist who participated in the study)

What About Palmdale?—The Antelope Valley News reminds us that Palmdale airport is there to relieve the burden on LAX, as part of a regional approach to airport planning. (Several newspaper articles and press releases)

1997 County Commissioned Poll—The county finds that the electorate does not back El Toro airport, nor trust county staff. (Public document)

2001 Cal State Fullerton Survey—March 2001 results plus summary of 4 previous surveys of public opinion. Airport opposition outnumbers support in North County. (Provided as e-mail by the university, upon request)

Twelve ETRPA Polls—April 2002 release of data from twelve previously private polls shows support for airport at its lowest level. (Report provided by the El Toro Reuse Planning Authority as a .pdf file)

Assembly Bill 1248—Bill to remove Orange County's special exemption from the California law, which requires voter approval of airport revenue bonds. (From state website)

Who Really Cares About El Toro?—A survey of who writes Letters to the Editors shows Newport Beach residents to be the leading boosters of an airport at El Toro. (Summary prepared by an activist from public library data)

The jetport is dead; long live the parks.—It took 7 years before efforts to turn Florida's Homestead AFB into a commercial airport finally died…a message for Orange County. (Miami Herald article picked up by a website viewer while travelling and then obtained from the newspaper's website)

Content that promotes participation

Our website's mission includes a charge to promote citizen participation. The **Get Involved** Section is constructed for that purpose. Most of the content is of local origin and is illustrative of what you might include in a site. The following is from the sub-homepage of this section.

The Case Against El Toro Airport—One-page summary for handouts, letters or talks.

Important Meetings—Dates of meetings you'll want to be sure to attend. A continuously updated community calendar of airport related events.

Groups—The major organizations opposed to an El Toro Airport. Join in!

Airport Officials Mailing List—Addresses and phone numbers to write, fax, call, and e-mail. Incorporates direct hypertext e-mail links to the most important addresses.

Write Letters to the Editor of local newspapers. E-mail addresses and hypertext links to the papers

Action for Homeowner Associations—Homeowner groups should protect their interests. Legal opinion on how HOAs can participate without violating their rules regarding political activities.

PTAs have a Role—Parent teacher groups can act to protect their children.

Clergymen Speak Out—Clergy organize and say there are moral issues to be addressed regarding the airport.

Aircraft Noise Complaints—Who to call about noisy planes overhead.

In addition, the **Elections Section**, a specialized part of the site during election campaigns, includes the following topics to encourage participation.

Initiative Facts—Initiative text, official ballot arguments by both sides, County Counsel and Auditor-Controller's impartial analyses, other Voters' Pamphlet material

Information in support of our position

Campaign Office—Address, map with directions and phone number

Information on making campaign contributions—By mail or by the website's credit card link.

Volunteer opportunities—Names and contact information for area captains.

Photo Album—Pictures of volunteers working for the campaign

Other anti-airport candidates to support.

Voting data from previous anti-airport campaigns.

Website policy on political endorsements—See the Chapter on the Mission Statement.

Campaign statements from anti-airport candidates

Full text documents

The El Toro Info Site is highly regarded for its online library. Full text documents comprise much of the content listed above. Some of this material comes to us by e-mail. Other content is available from web-sites operated by the FAA, the state, and universities.

When our source is a hard copy document we either retype it into a word processor or use a scanner with optical character recognition software.

A good example of how this enhances our reputation occurred after the County of Orange released a massive draft environmental impact report for the proposed airport two days before Christmas in 1999. The multi-volume report was placed on public library shelves. Additional copies cost hundreds of dollars each to purchase.

The limited availability made it difficult for citizens to study the reports and make timely comments as provided for under California's Environmental Quality Act.

Website team member John Santora laboriously scanned much of the report and posted it on our website.

On February 7, 2000 Editor Rick Reiff published this editorial in the pro-airport Orange County Business Journal:

On-Line Info
AS EVERYONE KNOWS I'M FOR THE PROPOSED EL TORO AIRPORT

But let me give an attaboy to Len Kranser, who operates the anti-airport El Toro Airport Info Site, for doing what the county has chosen not to do on its own El Toro web site. Kranser is putting the county's draft environmental impact report on-line[1].

It's been a mammoth undertaking for anti-airport volunteers Kranser [and Santora]. Unlike the county, which could have simply transferred the files from a word processor to its website, they've had to optically scan the report page by page. So far, they've entered about 1,500 pages of text, which leaves them several thousand to go. Kranser says he doubts they'll get it all done by the Feb. 22 deadline for public comment.

"The county could have done this easily. Shame on them," Kranser said.

County officials wonder what the fuss is about. They note that their site does carry a thorough summary of the EIR. (Kranser's site carries the same summary.) For the vast majority of citizens, county officials say, the summary provides all the information they'll want about El Toro in a comprehensible way. And county officials say

---

1.   The Business Journal and others use the hyphenated "on-line" but "online" is correct according to *Webster's New World Dictionary of Computer Terms*.

that much of the report makes little sense without the accompanying charts and graphics, which are difficult to download and would jam many computers. (Kranser agrees that many of the charts are memory eaters.)

But c'mon guys. Where there's a will there's a way, and it would have been a public service to make the entire report, or at least the text portion of it, available on-line for those who want to access it.

Once again, chalk up a PR win for the airport foes.

When the environmental report was finalized, the anti-airport El Toro Reuse Planning Authority (ETRPA) filed a lawsuit asking that the EIR be declared invalid. The suit, which is still working its way through the court process, cites violations of the California Environmental Quality Act (CEQA).

"The County has made a mockery of the environmental review process," said El Toro Reuse Planning Authority Chairman Allan Songstad. "The Supervisors decided to pick and choose what information to share with the public. They systematically ignored any data that cast a negative light on the airport plan. The result is an EIR that defies common sense."

Honest reporting builds credibility and viewership. That is how the fight for public opinion is won.

10

Using Federal and State Open Government Laws

A website like the El Toro Info Site collects most of its content by searching other Internet sources, scanning the conventional media, conversing with local leaders, and tapping other readily available sources. However, from an activist's standpoint some of the most exciting and valuable website content comes from harder-to-reach sources.

This chapter deals with investigative reporting tools for finding and publishing public records that were not really intended to be public. Political activists need to know how to utilize federal and state open government laws that enable citizens to access internal government documents.

These records fall into two general categories: federal documents available through the Freedom of Information Act (FOIA) and state and local documents available through what we will lump together as local public records laws.

Much of this chapter is dry reading about tedious procedures but I have interspersed success stories that illustrate why it pays to use these tools. Several of our document discoveries became major stories in the traditional media.

Using the U.S. Freedom of Information Act

The following paragraphs are excerpted from the El Toro Info Site where we published them in the **Get Involved Section** to encourage citizen participation. The federal government was the original source before editing.

Of particular importance is the paragraph reproduced in bold listing what information is exempt from disclosure. Government agencies may attempt to stretch the meaning of the exemptions to avoid disclosure. The activist-investigative reporter needs to be able to assert his or her rights to the records.

Freedom of Information Act

1. General Overview of the Freedom of Information Act (FOIA) and the Privacy Act

    The FOIA, enacted in 1966, provides that any person has the right to request access to federal agency records or information. Federal agencies are required to disclose records upon receiving a written request for them except for those records that are protected from disclosure by the nine exemptions and three exclusions of the FOIA. This right of access is enforceable in court. The FOIA covers all records in the possession and control of federal executive branch agencies.

    The Privacy Act is another federal law regarding federal government records or information about individuals. The Privacy Act establishes certain controls over how the executive branch agencies of the federal government gather, maintain, and disseminate personal information.

    The Privacy Act, passed by Congress in 1974, establishes certain controls over what personal information is collected by the federal government and how it is used. The act guarantees three primary rights: (1)the right to see records about oneself, subject to the Privacy Act's exemptions; (2)the right to amend that record if it is inaccurate, irrelevant, untimely, or incomplete; and (3)the right to sue the government for violations of the statute, including permitting others to see your records, unless specifically permitted by the act.

2. Guide for Freedom of Information Act Requesters

How do I request information under the FOIA?

Your request must be in writing, must state that you are requesting documents under the provisions of the Freedom of Information Act, and must be signed by the requester.

The request should describe the subject matter of an existing record, and, if known, indicate the date of the record, the place where it originated, and the name of the originating person or office.

Your letter must be specific as to which documents you are requesting under FOIA. The more information you can provide about the document, such as its author or date, the more expeditiously your request will be processed. Your request will be logged and a tracking number assigned to it. The tracking number assigned is of great importance to you as a requester, because in the event you would like to check the status of your request, the number enables the agency to locate where in the process your request is. When requesting information pertaining to a solicitation or contract, please include the appropriate solicitation or contract number for that record. This FOIA does not permit a requester to ask questions when seeking records under the Freedom of Information Act.

Your letter should include a statement of obligation to pay the administrative fees for processing your request.

To expedite handling, mark both your letter and the envelope "Freedom of Information Act Request."

As a general rule FOIA requesters are not required to state the reasons why they are making their requests. You may do so if you think it might help the agency to locate the records. If you are not sure whether the records you want are exempt from disclosure, you may request them anyway. Under certain circumstances agencies have the discretion to disclose exempt information and, in line with the government's openness policy, they are encouraged to do so whenever possible.

What information is available under the FOIA?

The FOIA provides access to all federal agency records (or portions of those records), except for those records that are protected from disclosure by nine exemptions and three exclusions (reasons for which an agency may withhold records from a requester).

The exemptions cover (1)classified national defense and foreign relations information, (2)internal agency rules and practices, (3)information that is prohibited from disclosure by another law, (4)trade secrets and other confidential business information, (5)inter-agency or intra-agency communications that are protected by legal privileges, (6)information involving matters of personal privacy, (7)certain information compiled for law enforcement purposes, (8)information relating to the supervision of financial institutions, and (9)geological information on wells. The three exclusions, which are rarely used, pertain to especially sensitive law enforcement and national security matters. Even if information is exempt from disclosure under the FOIA, the agency still may disclose it as a matter of administrative discretion when that is not prohibited by any law and would not cause any foreseeable harm.

What about costs for getting records under the FOIA?

The FOIA permits agencies to charge fees to FOIA requesters. For commercial requesters, an agency may charge for the cost of searching, reviewing, and excising for records and the cost of making copies. Search, review, and excising fees range from $12 to $45 per hour depending upon the salary levels of the personnel needed for the search. The charge for photocopying documents is $.15 per page and $.02 per page for pre-printed documents. For noncommercial requests, agencies will not charge for the first two hours of search time or for the first 100 pages of document copying. Administrative fees are automatically waived for FOIA request that do not exceed $15.00. The agency will notify you before proceeding with a request that will involve large fees, unless your request letter states your willingness to pay fees as large as that amount. **If fees are charged, you may request a waiver of fees if you can show that the records, when disclosed to you, will contribute significantly to the public's understanding of the operations or activities of the government.**

How does an agency make the determination of whether or not a record can be released?

The custodian of the records with the assistance of its organization's Freedom of Information and Privacy Act Office makes the determination whether the records can be released in accordance with the FOIA, its exemptions, and the agency's FOIA regulations.

How do I appeal a denial?

To appeal a denial, promptly send a letter to the agency. Your appeal must be made within 60 days after you receive notification of a denial. The denial letter will tell you the office to which your appeal letter should be addressed. For the quickest possible handling, you should mark both your request letter and the envelope "Freedom of Information Act Appeal."

To appeal, request that the agency review your FOIA request and its denial decision. Give your reason(s) for believing that the denial was wrong. Be sure to refer to any pertinent communications you have had with the agency on the request and include any number the agency may have assigned to your request. It can save time in acting on your appeal if you include copies of your FOIA request and the agency's denial letter. You do not need to enclose copies of any documents released to you. Under the FOIA, the agency has 20 working days (excluding Saturdays, Sundays, and federal holidays) to decide your appeal. Under certain circumstances, it may also take an extension of up to 10 working days.

Sample FOIA Request Letter

Date

Freedom of Information Act Request Agency Head or FOIA Officer Name of agency or agency component Address

Dear _____:

Under the Freedom of Information Act, 5 U.S.C. subsection 552, I am requesting access to [identify the records as clearly and specifically as possible].

If there are any fees for searching for or copying the records, please let me know before you fill my request. [Or, please supply the records without informing me of the cost if the fees do not exceed $_____, which I agree to pay.]

If you deny all or any part of this request, please cite each specific exemption you think justifies your refusal to release the information and notify me of appeal procedures available under the law.

Optional: If you have any questions about handling this request, you may telephone me at _____ (home phone) or at _____ (office phone).

Sincerely,

Name Address

Additional Sources of Information about the FOIA:

Citizens Guide on Using the Freedom of Information Act and the Privacy Act of 1974 to Request Government Records. This booklet, written by the Committee on Government Reform and Oversight, U.S. House of Representatives, provides a detailed explanation of the Freedom of Information Act and the Privacy Act. It may be purchased for $3.00 from the Superintendent of Documents, P.O.

Box 371954, Pittsburgh, PA 15250-7954. To order by telephone, call (202) 512-1800. The stock number is 052-071-01129-3.

Freedom of Information Act Guide and Privacy Act Overview. This book is updated annually (in mid-fall) by the Justice Department's Office of Information and Privacy. The *Justice Department's Guide to the Freedom of Information Act* is a comprehensive summary of the law that includes a discussion of the nine FOIA exemptions and its most important procedural aspects. *The Privacy Act Overview*, prepared in coordination with the Office of Management and Budget, is a discussion of the provisions of the Privacy Act. The book also contains the texts of both statutes. It may be purchased for $3.00 from the Superintendent of Documents, P.O. Box 371954, Pittsburgh, PA 15250- 7954. To order by telephone, call (202) 512-1800. The stock number is 052-071-01129-3. Text versions are also available on the Justice Department's website at **http://www.usdoj.gov/oip/**

Federal Information Center. The Federal Information Center (FIC), administered by the General Services Administration, can help you find information about the federal government's agencies, services, and programs. You may call the FIC for assistance in contacting the proper federal agency with your Freedom of Information Act or Privacy Act request.

Call 800-688-9889 toll-free from anywhere in the United States. Users of text telephones (TDD/TTY) may also call toll-free at 800-326-2996.

The FIC is open from 9 a.m. to 5 p.m., Eastern Time, except in Alaska (8 a.m. to 4 p.m.) and Hawaii (7 a.m. to 3 p.m.).

Fees

Note in the bold text above, that the federal agency can waive any fees "if you can show that the records, when disclosed to you, will contribute significantly to the public's understanding of the operations or activities of the government."

As a public website we have obtained thousands of pages of documents with the fees always waived. When approaching a new agency, we include the following lengthy statement in FOIA requests. It can be copied from our website and pasted into your letter to avoid retyping.

> The amended Act provides that search and reproduction fees be waived if it "is in the public interest because furnishing the information can be considered as primarily benefiting the public." I believe this request plainly fits that category.
>
> The requested records bear upon an issue of great public concern. Government officials, the media, and the public have all demonstrated interest in the proposed building of a commercial airport at the closing MCAS El Toro, as witnessed by the thousands of public comments submitted to the County of Orange during the circulation of Environmental Impact Report No. 563 (prepared for the Community Reuse Plan). The reuse of MCAS El Toro has been a topic of debate at the local and county level ever since the closure of MCAS El Toro was announced in 1993. As such, MCAS El Toro is substantiated as being one of the most important issues to Orange County citizens in this decade and has been the subject of two voter ballot initiatives. Citizens have an ongoing interest in the attitudes and interests of the government in dealing with the public on these issues. The requested records will benefit the public by clarifying issues related to Federal Aviation Administration's policies, procedures, actions, and activities relative to public use of closing military bases and the agencies involved in there reuse efforts.
>
> In determining that this request qualifies for a fee waiver, I make my case as follows:
>
> 1. Is disclosure of the information in the public interest?
>
> Clearly the answer to this question is **yes**. The information requested is likely to contribute significantly to public understanding of the operations or activities of the government and shall not be used in the commercial interest of the requester.

Proposals for reuse of closing military bases have stimulated a high degree of public and media interest. Clearly the closing/reuse issues surrounding MCAS El Toro are no exception. Disclosure of the requested information would contribute significantly to public understanding of the operations and activities of the Federal Aviation Administration in regard to this matter. In addition, the records are requested solely in the public interest and shall not be used for any commercial or financial interest.

2. Does the record concern the operations or activities of the government?

Clearly, the answer to this question is **yes**. My request plainly fits this category. As called for in the federal regulations, disclosure of this information has a direct bearing upon the manner in which your agency carries out its operations and activities and the manner in which these operations and activities affect the public. The connection between the records sought and the operations and activities of your agency are clear and direct.

3. If a record concerns the operations or activities of the government, is its disclosure likely to contribute to public understanding of these operations and activities?

Again, the answer is clearly **yes**. The content of the requested records relates directly to the operations and activities of your agency. I am the editor of a web site (accessible to the public—free of charge) which is dedicated to conducting on-going research and providing meaningful information as it relates to the closure, clean up, and reuse of MCAS El Toro. The reuse plan approved by the Local Redevelopment Authority (County of Orange) included the preparation of a state Environmental Impact Report (EIR No. 563), as well as the current preparation of a federal environmental impact study pursuant to the National Environmental Protection Act [NEPA]. My web site delves into discovering how the government participates in approval of such proposed reuse plans and into how both the local and federal government proceed with reuse plans as measured by their relationships with the public (how they carry out their activities, duties and actions and how they affect the public).

The connection between the records sought and the operations and activities of your agency are clear and direct. My web site presents the results of independent research and documentation to hundreds of people each month. The results of my request with the Federal Aviation Administration will be made available to the public without charge or user fee via the Internet.

The records I have requested are meaningfully informative of your agency's operations and activities as it relates to the proposed reuse plan for MCAS El Toro and interaction with public/private entities. The focus of my request is on the contribution to public understanding not individual understanding or the understanding of a narrow segment of interested persons. Matters of airports and aviation operations are of far reaching interest to the general public. The requested records deal with a well-publicized, long-standing, and controversial issue of enormous importance and public interest. My informational web site has been, and will continue to be, intimately involved with the subject of the requested records. My ability and intention to disseminate the information released through this request to the general public has been well demonstrated by my past and current involvement with this issue.

I seek this information because it is informative of government operations and activities. The requested records have no intrinsic value other than the light they may shed on government operations and activities.

Again, as an editor of a web site accessible to the general public free of charge, I have no commercial interest that would be furthered by the requested disclosure. The requested records do not appear to have any commercial value whatsoever and have nothing to do with commercial, trade, or profit interest. Rather than seeking profit, we seek to provide meaningful information to the general public through the Internet pertaining to the activities and actions of governmental agencies involved in the closure, clean up, and reuse of MCAS El Toro.

To summarize, my request clearly fulfills the fee waiver criteria set forth by the federal guidelines. Therefore, I request that you waive all search and reproduction fees.

This may appear to be a lot to include in a letter, but the sample text came to us from an experienced FOIA researcher and activist. After the first few requests to an agency I employ a much shorter version that essentially says, "You have waived the fees for our use in similar past instances."

A FOIA success story

The effort can pay off. On November 12, 1999 the following article appeared in the El Toro website news.

FAA Documents Expose Concerns Over El Toro Plans

The FAA has provided internal documents that reveal substantial concern amongst key officials regarding El Toro plans. The documents, mostly internal memos and e-mail, were released in response to a Freedom of Information Act (FOIA) request filed by this website and just made public. The documents reveal FAA managers raising pointed concerns about the management of crowded airspace around the base—and about possible future operations at El Toro.

The news article included a link to a website page recapping documents received for the period from May to August 1999. This was a time period when the county arranged a series of demonstration flights at El Toro. County officials hoped to convince the public that the overflights would not be objectionably loud.

In several unusually frank e-mail exchanges, FAA managers argued over the county proposal to conduct the flights.

One FAA manager writes to another, "Personally, I find it ludicrous that as an organization we would stand idly by while a local government agency with no Federal authority over airspace negotiates some undefined demonstration project with a host of air carriers."

Another characterizes the purpose of the flight demonstration.

"Here's the issue as I see it…Orange County Board of Supervisors is generally split 3/2 in favor of the airport. The citizenry is about 50% split pro/con on the airport. The flight demos are being propounded by the pro group as a way to demonstrate the noise issue. If the noise isn't terribly obtrusive (and we know that the carriers will fly as quiet as possible…) the pro group will say 'I told you so.'"

After the demonstration, a manager writes,

"Especially after our experience with the flight demonstration, I am concerned that the Airports Division is not going to let us comment on anything to do with El Toro. Thus we may eventually be stuck with an airport layout that, while it looks great by itself on paper, is virtually unusable from an integrated ATC [Air Traffic Control] standpoint….I do not look forward to the years of safety problems and litigation we might undergo as we work to fix a bad initial plan."

The website provided 30 pages of such documents to a friendly reporter at the Orange County Register, the county's most read newspaper. The payoff from this piece of document research came when the Register ran a front-page above-the-fold story the following day with the following five-column wide headline.

FAA officials split on El Toro
E-mails surrounding June tests reveal worries over safety.

The resulting newspaper coverage was a major boost for the anti-airport side in the battle over El Toro. To some extent the FAA revelations marked a turning point for public opinion on the issue. The report also provided a boost for the prestige of the website. Many new viewers came to read more details of the e-mails online. Thousands of newspaper subscribers became aware of our site through this report.

Handing off the story to the newspaper is an example of how we build a good working relationship with our professional friends in the traditional media.

The FAA never again provided documents that were so revealing. On January 21, 2001 the Los Angeles Times ran an op-ed article that I wrote. The headline and an excerpt said:

FAA Builds a Stone Wall Around El Toro

The aviation agency is an ally of airport supporters, and it helps by withholding public information.

Since 1998 I have submitted 11 Freedom of Information Act (FOIA) requests to the FAA on behalf of Orange County residents. Bureaucrats have stonewalled, and documents that could shed light on the plans for El Toro and John Wayne are systematically withheld.

Using state open-government laws

We are fortunate in California to have the Public Records Act. It requires disclosure of documents in the possession of state, county, city, and other governmental agencies. It goes a step further than the federal FOIA law by setting a time limit for production of the documents. While federal disclosure may drag out for six months or longer, a California Public Records Request must be answered in ten days unless certain circumstances allow a brief additional delay.

Many states have similar laws. For information on your state contact the Citizen Access Project operated out of the University of Florida's College of Journalism and Communications. The website is at **http:// www.citizenaccess.org/**

Another source of information on federal and state laws is the National Freedom of Information Coalition built by the Bechner Center for Freedom of Information and the Society of Professional Journalists. The website is **http://www.nfoic.org/web/index.htm**

A California Public Records Act success story

On July 9, 2001 the website posted a new page titled **SCAG Calculation Error.** The page summarized 15 e-mail messages exchanged between the editor of the website and representatives of the Southern California Association of Governments, SCAG. SCAG is responsible for regional transportation planning.

The agency's most recent regional plan stated that residents and visitors from Orange County had taken 16 million airplane trips in 2000 and were predicted to take 30 million in 2020. This would require a new airport at El Toro.

When I asked for the source of the 16 million annual passengers (MAP) figure the agency replied.

> "SCAG data [was] derived from over 60,000 air passenger surveys taken at all six air carrier airports in the region as well as at Lindbergh Field in San Diego."

That prompted me to send this response to SCAG.

> "The El Toro Airport website collects and Internet publishes information regarding El Toro reuse. We have information from only two surveys of passengers on our website."

> "It would be appreciated if you could identify the six surveys referred to in the response with title, date, and a contact to facilitate my obtaining copies."

I was referred to the SCAG legal department. After several contacts with their lawyer, I finally resorted to the Public Records Act.

> "This message from SCAG does not answer my inquiry. The evasive response only raises new questions as to why the information is being withheld."

"...Furthermore, in light of your e-mail, I now also request copies of all SCAG documents and calculations used to develop the 16 MAP estimate of Orange County demand from the referenced survey data, and copies of any report to SCAG, from [consultants], dealing with this matter."

"Please accept this e-mail as a request under the California Records Act. A complete and prompt response will be appreciated. Thank you."

Ten working days later I telephoned and e-mailed SCAG's attorney, in part as follows:

"It has been 10 working days since I filed a request with you, on June 5 under the California Public Records Act. I called to ascertain your intentions regarding the response to my request..."

SCAG e-mailed back, the same day, in part:

"...Due to pending litigation against SCAG related to the El Toro airport matter...SCAG is unable to provide you with records you are requesting. The California Public Records Act provides exceptions for 'proprietary data' and for 'records pertaining to pending litigation'...."

Based on information contained in a California website operated by the First Amendment Coalition, **http://www.thefirstamendment.org/** I was able to respond in part:

"I believe that the exception may apply to attorney-client or attorney work product but not to other documents for a project whose approval results in a lawsuit. I believe that public records remain public records. It is difficult to understand why this material, which is of great public interest, is being withheld."

SCAG finally relented and provided whatever data existed. An analysis revealed the planners had misapplied information from a consultant. By multiplying the wrong two numbers, the regional planning agency has estimated 16 million annual passengers. Under persistent questioning, a planner admitted that the correct figure was closer to 12 MAP.

The Los Angeles Times ran it as a major story day on the same day the information was posted on the El Toro Info Site. We had provided a lead reporter with all of the relevant communications in advance with the following dramatic results.

LA Times, July 9, 2001

Air Passenger Count for O.C. 33% Too High

Regional agency concedes it overestimated county travelers in 2000 by 4 million. The higher figure has been used to argue for a new airport.

Regional airport officials have acknowledged that they overestimated by 4 million the number of airline passengers leaving or heading to Orange County—a number that supporters have used to justify plans for an airport at the closed El Toro Marine base. The Southern California Assn. of Governments [SCAG] estimated in a report approved in May that Orange County accounted for 16 million of the 89 million passengers using Southern California airports in 2000.

The actual number of Orange County travelers using all airports in 2000 was 12 million, SCAG aviation planner Mike Armstrong said last week. About 7 million Orange County passengers traveled through John Wayne. That left LAX and Ontario picking up the remaining 5 million, he said.

'It was an oversight,' he said of the 16-million figure, which was included in SCAG's report in response to questions from El Toro anti-airport activist Len Kranser.

The Orange County Register, which had not done an immediate story, joined in a couple of days later with this headline:

OC Register, July 11, 2000

Airport foes say panel overstated O.C. demand

4 million phantom passengers cause confusion.

It is great when a community website can provide hot news. However, the real power of the Internet arises from being able to reach out beyond the online community to a much broader audience. This was the case with the two examples discussed above.

11

Creating Relationships with the News Media

As discussed in the previous chapter, if you have important news, you eventually will want to share it with the larger universe that does not come to the website. After all, an activist's objective is to influence the outcome of a community issue and not just to build a great website. This chapter adds more suggestions about getting material into the traditional media news.

Working with reporters

On an issue as large as the reuse of El Toro, the newspapers regularly turn to one or two of their reporters whenever a story comes up. These reporters know the subject matter, and they know the people. They are at the important meetings. Some of them may cover little else. It is their beat.

If reporters regularly cover your issue, it is important to develop a working relationship with them. In the course of writing stories, a good reporter will try to make a balanced presentation covering both sides of a contentious subject. That means you have an opportunity to input your viewpoint.

Activists frequently complain that they don't get to say their piece. Several anti-airport groups in other states claim local government officials and special interests have the newspapers in their pockets. Whether that is true or not, it is a common perception.

Your task is to make sure that your viewpoint is included. One way to do this is by developing a mutually beneficial working relationship with the media. Be useful to reporters. Their job is to write stories, and you can help.

In the chapter on using the Freedom of Information Act, I've given examples of a couple of big stories that were delivered to newspaper reporters on a platter. More often, what will help them to do their job is something very much simpler. They may call seeking:

- Names and numbers for volunteers who they can interview for a new angle

- A piece of factual data

- Background information

- A quote

Many newspapers like to liven up their stories by including quotes from individuals involved in the matter being covered. The reporter has his or her story almost done but needs that extra human touch. They frequently don't want a big explanation when they call and ask, "What's your comment on…?"

What works is a "sound bite" or two. Read the papers and you will see how often individuals are quoted in just a single sentence. Your task is constantly to think about your issue and always to be ready with that zinger sentence when asked for it.

A great example was provided by Meg Waters, a highly successful media consultant for the group of cities opposed to the airport. When asked recently about a plan being proposed for new runway layouts and flight paths at El Toro she snapped out, "It has something for everyone to hate." She was right on the mark.

When Meg, who is a good friend, heard that I was writing this book, she reminded me of another memorable line—her 1998 quip to a reporter. Back then, I'd complained that it was unnecessary to launch another website on our issue, and Meg said, "Len has his knickers in a twist, because he wants to own the whole Internet when it comes to El Toro." She also added, to her own chagrin, "I don't give an (expletive) if there are twenty websites." The original expletive appeared in print. Be colorful but careful with what you say to reporters.

Not all issues are big enough to have regular reporters assigned. If you are concerned with matters that do not occupy any one reporter for much of their time, then your task becomes one of bringing them up to speed. You have to explain the situation in the sort of simplified outline that characterizes newspaper stories. Be prepared to connect the dots for someone who lacks your background familiarity. Avoid using technical jargon. Don't assume the other party understands what seems like second nature to you. A good reporter will catch on quickly as long as you clearly organize the explanation.

One technique for doing this is to steer the reporter to webpages supporting the points you want to make. I do this often by sending e-mail with hypertext links to our pages imbedded in the message.

Subject: El Toro Sale Puts Regional Plans in a Fix

The El Toro Info Site **http://www.eltoroairport.org** has been collecting and reporting information about area airports since 1996.

Several relevant reports are contained in the Issues subsection on Aviation Demand.
http://www.eltoroairport.org/issues.html#demand

In particular, I recommend reading the review on Aviation Forecasts that summarizes past gross errors in SCAG estimates. **http://www.eltoroairport.org/issues/forecasts.html**

In another section on Safety and Flight Paths, **http://www.eltoroairport.org/issues.html#safety** you will find considerable information on the problematic location of El Toro, adjacent to mountains and in crowded airspace. Regardless of any politician's desire for regional solutions, El Toro is not a suitable location for a major commercial airport.

We would be pleased to assist you with research material for any future articles on this subject.

While some people might take offense at being corrected, most reporters are anxious to have good information in their stories. The above message produced this reply.

Hi Leonard. Thanks for sending along these links. I'll take a look at them. I agree with you that forecasting aviation demand accurately is a sticky prospect, at best. Unfortunately, SCAG's numbers are the only tools we have right now to discuss how demand may be spread out among the region's airports. But I do think it would be useful to do a story about SCAG's track record in aviation forecasting so readers know what to make of these statistics. I'm working on such a piece now.

The flow of information goes two ways. Reporters with whom we work help us by e-mailing articles or faxing documents they have which we need for the website.

Press releases

Press releases are documents sent to one or more news outlets providing material for a story. There are several rules for producing a good press release that increase its chances of being used. Here are a few of the most important:

• Provide contact information in the heading of the release.

• In the opening paragraph, answer the questions as to who, what, when, where, and why.

- Write in the same style used by the newspaper, so the person using your release does not have to rewrite it to remove wordiness, flowery or passionate language, or to fix the grammar.

- Restrain your partisanship and write impartially as the newspaper must and not as you wish they would.

- Put all controversial statements and hyperbole into the mouth of a spokesperson as a quote. That way the spokesperson and not the newspaper is responsible for the statement. Quotes also suggest the flavor you hope will show in the final article.

- Add some filler material at the end of the release that provides background information but easily can be deleted when the article is cut to fit.

The following is an example of a release that follows these guidelines and fits nicely on one page for faxing. Note how a spokesman is used. In this and many situations the writer of the press release works with the person who makes the statement so that they complement each other.

Some organizations especially in radio and TV like faxes that can be passed around, but reporters are becoming more accepting of releases by e-mail.

FOR IMMEDIATE RELEASE

Contact Information: Len Kranser (Phone number included)
Editor@eltoroairport.org

O.C. PROPERTY TAX REVENUE WILL DROP $35 MILLION IF EL TORO AIRPORT IS BUILT

OC business and homeowners could suffer a $3.5 billion loss in equity

IRVINE—January 23, 2002—Larry Bales, a candidate for Orange County Assessor, will make a presentation at tonight's El Toro Reuse Planning Authority (ETRPA) board meeting stating that the proposed El Toro airport will cost Orange County business and home owners as much as $3.5 billion in lost equity. This could double the cost of the airport project. Based on this potential dramatic loss in property value, the County General Fund could face a $35 million annual loss in property tax revenue if an airport at El Toro is built.

The report is based on several noise impact studies including an analysis commissioned by the Federal Aviation Administration and the County's own Environmental Impact Report 573. Bales' report cites the FAA finding that the value of a residence decreases by 1.33 percent for every decibel of airport noise. The report also states that "the value of a house and lot increases by about 3.4 percent for every quarter of a mile the house is farther away from being directly underneath the flight track of a departing / approaching jet aircraft."

According to Bill Kogerman, Chairman of the Yes on W campaign for the Orange County Central Park and Nature Preserve Initiative, "Pro-airport supervisor Cynthia Coad lamented that it might cost the county general fund $1-2 million per year to support public educational and recreational use of the former base. Where does the county expect to recoup the $35 million dollar annual loss to the general fund from the airport? What programs will they cut?"

The report includes only noise impacts and does not factor in pollution, traffic or general urban blight that typically occurs near airports.

The ETRPA board meeting will be held tonight at Lake Forest City Hall at 6:00 p.m. The address for City Hall is 23161 Lake Center Dr. Suite 100, Lake Forest.

The entire report is online at **http://www.eltoroairport.org/ issues/taxloss.html**.

#

Despite the well-written release, this story received little attention from the press. You win some and lose some.

12

Reaching the Wide World Beyond the Web

More people get their news from the newspapers and television than from the World Wide Web though reliance on the latter is growing.

Of the people who express interest in receiving more information about our issue and supply a snail mail address, only about 20 percent also provide an e-mail address. The challenge for the Internet activist is how to use the 20 percent to reach and influence the remaining 80 percent.

There are several means to do this. The previous chapters discuss working with the media to incorporate our message. Another important way to reach the general public is by word of mouth. Well-informed website viewers share information with others. They tend to be opinion leaders. Voters are more likely to rely on information from friends, neighbors, and associates whom they trust rather than on campaign literature and television ads.

Webpages as handouts

Webpage handouts are useful for reaching people beyond the web. Documents posted on our website are frequently printed by viewers and distributed as handouts at meetings.

For example, the El Toro Info Site provides summaries of several international studies on the adverse effects of aircraft noise on children.

Printouts of these documents circulated at school board meetings, often in the packets of material provided to the board members by their staffs and associates. Several school districts eventually took official positions of opposition to the airport, citing these reports of adverse impacts on children's health and their learning as the reason.

A classic illustration is the following message sent to presidents of all of the Parent Teacher Student Associations (PTSAs) in the large Capistrano Unified School District. It cites a Cornell report and other studies published and distributed by our website:

For Immediate Release for all PTSA Newsletters

From: Capistrano Unified Council of PTSAs Legislation

Subject: El Toro Airport Proposal Flies in a Cloud of Controversy

Controversy clouds daily over the proposed international commercial airport at the El Toro Marine base. Daily newspaper editorials and articles have us all scratching our heads trying to decipher who is right and who is wrong. As PTSA members our main concern about the proposed airport is how it will affect our children.

Recently on June 9th, our Capistrano Unified School District trustees voted unanimously to oppose construction of a commercial airport at El Toro. Their resolution was based on studies concerning the negative impacts of aircraft noise and pollution on children. Studies, such as the one recently published by Cornell University, showed a direct correlation between chronic noise, such as those produced by airports, and the children's ability to recognize and understand spoken words. Reading scores in areas near airports were reported lower than those in quieter areas. According to researchers, the reason for low reading scores was because kids tune out speech in noisy areas.

On Wednesday, September 10, the Capistrano Unified Council of PTSAs also voted on behalf of all our school children to oppose the construction of a commercial airport at El Toro, and to support the study of non-aviation uses that would benefit our communities.

The federal government is currently conducting their own study of reuses for El Toro. It is critical that this study also includes non-aviation ideas and proposals. You can write to them and express your opinion, pro or con, on the commercial airport, or offer any suggestions you may have for non-aviation use of the El Toro Marine base.

To facilitate such distribution of information as handouts, try, where practical, to publish abstracts or format reports so they can be printed on one or two pages.

Letters to the Editor

Considerable website information also flows to the general public through letters to the editors of newspapers. There are over 30 local daily and weekly newspapers and magazines in Orange County.

The El Toro Info Site publishes their e-mail addresses in our **Newspaper E-mail List** page. We incorporate hypertext links to these addresses in the webpage.

The syntax or HTML format for the link is
mailto:ocletters@latimes.com with no spaces.

Viewers need only visit the page and click on a link to open an e-mail message block to the newspaper of their choice. Many viewers send their messages to multiple papers by copying and pasting.

We remind viewers of the importance of writing to the papers. In news stories, we often include a link to the paper that originated it. This is especially the case when we believe that the newspaper reporter or editorial writer has taken an improper position.

We may start a Message Board thread with the text of a newspaper article and the e-mail address of the paper. We encourage viewers to write to the paper and also to post their letters on the Board to be read by other website viewers.

In one such instance a San Diego County newspaper published an editorial criticizing the voters of Orange County for rejecting the El

Toro airport. In a Message Board thread entitled **San Diego Butts In,** several viewers posted excellent letters. Three of them were subsequently printed in the paper.

This letter published in the Los Angeles Times shortly after the March 2002 election summarizes the importance of good information to public understanding. The writer, Todd Thornton, is an airline pilot, website viewer, and active participant in the grass roots effort against the county's airport plan.

> The driving force behind El Toro was always Newport Beach's big-money interests, who, fed up with aircraft noise from John Wayne Airport, wanted to move commercial jet service to El Toro. Cramming a giant airport down the throats of south Orange County residents was the end game.
>
> South County residents were fighting a corrupt planning process that was intent on concealing noise, pollution, and traffic impacts from an El Toro airport. The more people became informed about the proposed airport, the more they realized what was taking place.

On the same day the Times ran Thornton's letter, the OC Register's editorial page published the following Quote of the Day:

> Let the people know the truth and the country is safe.—Abraham Lincoln

Tips on writing letters to the editors.

As an activist you will want to speak out in more places than just on the Internet. You will be collecting a lot of information and should share it as broadly as possible. Writing letters to the papers is one such means for sharing your opinion with a wider audience.

Here are a few tips from my experience gained in the course of getting dozens of letters published.

- Be brief. Shorter letters have the best chance of being printed. Edit your words and use them frugally. Do the same on the website and in e-mails.

- Send your letter immediately by e-mail if commenting on something written in the paper. Controversial issues generate numerous letters, and the first ones received may be the ones used.

- When responding to an article, editorial, or prior letter writer, don't expect readers to remember what was said. Provide your own capsule summary.

- Avoid repeating an opponent's best argument for him. It is bad enough if the opposition makes its point once, don't make it a second time just the way he intended it and thereby reinforce it. Frame the original statement so it loses some of its impact.

- Don't use sarcasm or a writing style where the intended meaning depends on how the words are spoken. Without the benefit of your voice inflection, your letter could be confusing.

- Avoid acronyms and terms that are not universally understood.

- Don't assume the reader knows the subjects as well as you do. Your letter should be able to make sense to a marginally informed audience.

- Use humor or useful facts to make the letter interesting.

- Be crystal clear as to your intended point. Letters ending with a question to the reader fail to deliver a strong message. Sock it to them at the end.

I particularly enjoyed submitting this letter which appeared in several papers. I wrote it following a pitch for El Toro airport written by the then Chairman of the Board of Supervisors. It illustrates several of the above points.

> Board of Supervisors Chairman Charles Smith has a curious ratio-nale for wanting to squeeze an international airport into Orange County. He is quoted recently as saying that in terms of "gross national product," Orange County is equivalent to Greece or Por-tugal. "Can you imagine Greece or Portugal existing without an international airport?" Smith asked.
>
> Of course, Greece covers 51,146 square miles and Portugal occu-pies 36,390 square miles. It's several hundred miles and a day's drive or more across the border to the capital of the next friendly county. By contrast, Orange County occupies a mere 798 square miles. It's 39 miles by freeway from downtown Santa Ana to Los Angeles International Airport.
>
> If Smith wants us to copy Greece and Portugal, we will also need a major seaport, an airforce, navy, our own language and we should issue Orange County postage stamps.
>
> A country may need an international airport—but each U.S. county does not.

Supervisor Smith subsequently repeated the line in a couple of pub-lic forums with poor results. He eventually stopped using it.

The online and offline communities

Drop a stone into a pool of water and the energy disseminates outward in ever expanding circular ripples. The analogy applies to the dissemi-nation of information.

The website is at the epicenter. An online community of well-informed citizens occupies the first circle, and collects and relays infor-mation outward. Interactive Internet bulletin boards distribute the message. Information is copied and pasted from one document to another. E-mails are forwarded to long lists of recipients. The Internet is uniquely suited to this job. No other media performs the function as well.

A larger circle of partially connected citizens surrounds the online community. They receive e-mail, but rarely visit the originating websites. They scan the newspaper headlines and watch TV news, but learn most about the issues from their better-informed neighbors.

Beyond them lies the largest circle containing the majority of the population. They glance at political mail, hear what others are saying, and notice who endorses what position. They vote based on impressions that filter through to them.

The goal of the activist on the Internet is to originate messages that eventually penetrate to this offline outer circle. Thus we influence the wide world beyond the web.

13

Whistles and Bells and Fancy Stuff

This chapter deals with predominantly non-text elements of a website. These whistles and bells include graphics, photos, animations, audio clips, video content, counters, specially designed printouts, and links to other sites.

In general, inclusion of these items may make the site look jazzier, but they take time for viewers to download and contribute little to the success of the issue with which the site is dealing. There are some exceptions that will be discussed.

We use some graphics like the Info Site logo that appears on most pages plus a few icons in key spots to get attention. One such icon is placed where we ask viewers to click and subscribe to our e-mail list.

We try to include logos of organizations like the AirLine Pilots Association when we post their letters. We acquire these graphics from the organizations' webpages.

Over the years we drastically reduced the number of graphics associated with our homepage in order to make it load faster for our audience. As we have become better known for the usefulness of our content, we have seen less need to decorate our site. Beauty is only skin deep even on the Internet.

Graphics

We rarely use graphics as a decorative element except as noted above. We use them for informational purposes. The El Toro Info Site posts maps of the former Marine base, reuse plans, and flight paths. We include photos of elected officials who support our position. We depict volunteers at work, because this has a motivational benefit.

All of our graphics files are lodged in one directory on the site. That facilitates using them in multiple pages. When we create a new page we include a link to any image that we require.

It is preferable to use small size GIF or JPEG image files for easy loading. Files under 10 kilobytes are ideal. Over 35 KB is big by our standards.

When we need a graphic like a logo for a letterhead or a photo of an official, we "harvest" it from an appropriate website. We locate what we need on a site, right mouse click on the graphic, and save it to our images file with a name that will make sense to us in the future. We do not appropriate commercial graphics where copyrights apply.

Animations

These are special graphics that move, and they take more file space than static graphics. For years our trademark was an airplane that zoomed out of the distinctive black background of our homepage towards the viewer. It was as intrusive as the real aircraft we sought to block from our communities. A reporter with the OC Register referred to it as our "MTV look". Many viewers hated it.

After passing Measure W to kill the airport, we changed our name from the El Toro Airport website to the El Toro Info Site and deleted the airplane animation. No one complained.

We retain a couple of animations for entertainment, not including them in webpages but e-mailing them to friends and allies. They are primarily for poking fun at the county government.

One animation remains on our site. It is an aircraft noise simulator that superimposes, on a map of the county, the radius of noise impact from landing and departing airplanes. We got it from another anti-airport website in Indianapolis with their cooperation. John Santora, our webmaster, put a lot of work into modifying it for our purposes. We used it to spoof the county's real flight demonstration that cost taxpayers over a million dollars for aircraft rentals.

FREE AIRCRAFT NOISE DEMO

THIS DEMONSTRATION WILL PROVIDE MORE NON-SCIENTIFIC INFORMATION FOR FREE THAN THE COUNTY PROVIDES FOR $3 MILLION.

The members of the Board of Supervisors plan to spend $3 million of public funds to fly several aircraft in and out of El Toro. They have called this a "non-scientific snapshot" of the noise that will be produced by a 24 hour a day airport.

The FAA has NOT approved the aircraft flight paths that will be demonstrated. They are opposed, as unsafe, by the AirLine Pilots Association.

The aircraft that will be used by the county will not be fully loaded. Therefore, they will not demonstrate maximum noise.

Save $3 million with the website's flight demo—available 24 hours a day. Click here.

After the county flight demonstration turned into a noisy public relations fiasco, we were too proud of our simulator to take it down. Anyone interested in it will find it at **http://www.eltoroairport.org/simulator/jetnoiseeltoro.html**

Photos

There are three sources for photos. Scoop them from other websites, giving care to copyright regulations; scan them from photo prints, or shoot them with a digital camera.

When scanning, 70 dpi (dots per inch) is adequate website quality. To go higher will only yield big files but no appreciable improvement in appearance.

Viewers may e-mail digital photos. Sometimes these are huge files suitable for photo enlargements but too big for website use. Microsoft Photo Editor is one of several options for reducing the file down to a more workable size of 30-40Kb.

We post thumbnail miniatures of the pictures, in our photo album webpages, linked to the full sized version. That way, our page looks like a stamp album, loads quickly, and viewers still can click on the thumbnail to see a screen-filling version of any picture that interests them.

For a couple of sample pages see:

An Afternoon at John Wayne Airport

http://www.eltoroairport.org/issues/jwaphotos.html

Volunteers for the Central Park

http://www.eltoroairport.org/elections/campaign-photos.html

Audio clips

Please don't greet visitors to your site with the noise of a roaring airplane as one anti-airport site did, or martial music, or any other sound effect. It's a big file to load, and it gets tiresome after the first visit.

The time to use audio is when you can air a live interview with someone saying something newsworthy and important to your issue. We did it once, and it worked very well.

During the 2000 campaign, when the voters of Orange County passed their first anti-airport initiative, the District Attorney opposed the measure. Two years later, when he was running for reelection, we sensed that he might take a more popular position towards our second initiative. If so, it would be good for him and good for our cause.

We set up for a taped interview. I supplied the questions that would be asked, in advance, including one about how he intended to vote on the upcoming anti-airport Measure W. There is no point in not allowing an interviewee to prepare his or her best response.

With the help of volunteer and audio-engineer Dave Kirkey we taped an 11-minute interview. Dave used professional quality equipment and posted the interview on his own business website. Our own web host did not provide that type of capability, and it was just as easy to link to the site of someone who knew how to do the job.

We ran the story and the link to the interview at a carefully chosen point in the election campaign.

Website report, February 14, 2002

District Attorney says he will vote for Measure W

In a taped interview that can be heard on this website, District Attorney Anthony Rackauckas tells Website Editor Len Kranser that he personally "is going to vote in favor of Measure W," the OC Central Park and Nature Preserve initiative.

He states that he understands the problems of "fighting against the awesome power of those who are in control of the government." Rackauckas says it is "important that the voters decide a quality of life issue like having an airport," as opposed to it being decided by "a few people who have an economic interest."

The interview also discusses the inactivity of the Grand Jury relative to questionable County actions in the El Toro reuse process.

The newspapers picked up the story. The LA Times headline read:

Rackauckas Says He's for Great Park at El Toro.

There is no way to judge the total impact, but it seemed like a very useful way to employ Internet audio to augment our content.

Video clips

Several years ago we conducted videotaped interviews with two county supervisors. It was a great deal of trouble, and the quality was poor for viewers with slow modems. The online interviews got us a newspaper mention because they were a novelty at the time. Apart from that the content did nothing for our cause. I doubt we would do it again.

Printouts

Pages that can be downloaded and printed by viewers have a number of good uses.

In some cases petitions can be distributed this way. This is particularly true of petitions that do not have to meet stringent legal requirements since different viewer's printers may give differently sized results. In California petitions for election purposes are very rigidly specified as to type size and character weight.

We have posted a few flyers. Some announce events and some promote the website. One of the most useful is a single-page "**Case Against El Toro Airport**".

Activists have requested graphics that can be printed out for badges, buttons, banners, and store signs.

In one case we posted a contribution envelope that could be printed, cut, and folded.

We made a paper airplane imprinted like a $100 bill to highlight the wasted money being spent on the airport. The idea came from the anti-airport cities' consultants who used it in a print ad.

Regular html files will print out any which way depending on the viewer's browser and printer. If precision or uniformity is needed, the graphic will have to be posted as a pdf file and users will need Adobe Acrobat to download it.

Visitor counters and calendars

Been there and done that. Why bother? Only two viewers complained when we removed the date in order to simplify our homepage. It didn't influence whether the airport got built or not.

If you must have a calendar or counter, there are lots of programs for this available at the CGI Resource Center website at **http:// cgi.resourceindex.com/**

Polls

This is getting into much work for dubious benefits. The El Toro Info Site did one by e-mail but the sample was very unrepresentative of any other population. The volunteer-run Chronicles website, which will be discussed later, has polling software in place but finds it to be a lot of trouble to configure for each poll.

Several programs for polling and surveys also are available for little or no cost at the CGI Resource Center website, but you have the technical work of setting it up. **http://cgi.resourceindex.com/ Programs_and_Scripts/Perl/Survey_and_Voting/**

The local newspapers use website polls, and they are relatively easy to fool. In one much-publicized flap, leading airport supporters corrupted a Los Angeles Times poll and were caught. We gained more from the incident than they did.

Website Report, February 21, 2002—updated

OCRAA head involved in pro-airport effort to distort poll

A February 20 e-mail to Art Bloomer, Executive Director of the Orange County Airport Authority, OCRAA, provides instructions on how to distort an LA Times online poll regarding El Toro reuse. "If you want to vote multiple times…you can fool the computer," it reads.

Bloomer's e-mail to a large group of pro-airport associates, urging them to vote in the poll, was responded to by one of his addressees who furnished technical instructions on how to delete files that "tell the LA Times computer that you have already voted."

"Vote early and often", the e-mail urges.

Messages to the website team

Almost from the start we provided an e-mail hyperlink so our viewers could ask questions. Answering thousands of messages has required a lot of work, but it is a valuable communications and motivation tool.

No matter how much information is on the website individual viewers have their own personal questions. The most recurrent has been "Where will the flight paths be in relation to my house?"

Sometime all they need is to be pointed to the appropriate webpage for an answer. Sometimes it is a longer inquiry about anti-airport strategy or how the campaign money is being spent. Viewers offer suggestions.

Sometimes we receive very hostile pro-airport messages.

I responded in the beginning, but needed help as we grew in viewership. John Berry, a website team member with an outstanding understanding of the facts and issues, took over answering all of the e-mail.

Chat

At one point we opened a chat room enabling viewers to exchange real-time written comments with the editor. This gimmick generated little interest. From our experience, message boards are a better medium for exchanging ideas and information.

Links

Many issues-oriented websites include links to relevant resources at other sites. Hardcore activists use them for research.

Our **Links** page receives about one-half of one percent of the total hits on our site, probably from a small group of people who use the page like an address book, or in lieu of setting bookmarks to the other local airport websites. I do that.

We provide links to several categories of websites:

- El Toro reuse websites—pro- and anti-airport

- Airport Community Groups around the world

- Orange County and City Websites

- State and Federal Government Sites

- Watchdog Groups

- Other Area Airports

The major traffic is probably to the other El Toro websites. We have no problem with sending viewers to our competition for a well-rounded exposure to the arguments on this issue.

Some people believe it is polite to request permission before linking to another site. The alternate view is that they are out there looking for viewers and couldn't possibly object if you sent them a few. If you feel inclined to ask before linking, ask them for a reciprocal link back to your site.

14

Search Engines

A link on the El Toro Info Site homepage leads to a page incorporating the Google search engine. It is excellent, free, and adds real value to the site. The engine gives viewers the choice of searching our website or the entire World Wide Web.

I use it all the time to locate content I know we have covered on our site but which I can't find otherwise.

Put Google on the site

To add this capability to your site, contact Google at **http://www.google.com** and click on the links to sign up for the free version. We have "co-branded" the search page with our logo as Google suggests. See **http://www.eltoroairport.org/google/google-search.html**

Google summarizes their Free WebSearch and SiteSearch as follows:

> Google's WebSearch enables your site visitors to search the Internet. With Google's Free WebSearch, you can co-brand search results with your color scheme and logo.

> The optional Free SiteSearch enables you to restrict searches to the domain(s) you specify.

> Note: The free SiteSearch option is a sub-index of Google's main index. Updates are determined by Google and there is no guarantee of pages crawled.

Unlimited queries Free: The award-winning search is free, but Google reserves the right to serve ads on the search result pages

Co-branding: Your logo can be displayed above the search box in the header of the results page

Customization: You can customize all the key aspects of the results page including the background, link properties, text properties and many other elements

Fast installation: Have search up and running in less than five minutes

Optional SiteSearch: Enable your users to search your site with Google's optional SiteSearch

Searching for information.

To determine which search engine works best for researching your topic of interest, submit the same sample searches to several you like, and rate them for the quality of what they find. They all will deliver substantial numbers of referrals. My favorite engines are Google, Wisenut, and Copernic, in that order, but there are many others that I have yet to try.

Google is excellent for issues-oriented research. It does a particularly good job of finding newspaper and magazine articles. Since it is part of the El Toro Info Site, it is always close at hand.

Wisenut has replaced Yahoo in by bookmarks. Yahoo's popup ads became too annoying. This engine at **http://www.wisenut.com** produces the most matches, which is not necessarily good, but it puts good stuff on top.

Copernic is a search engine that goes out to other engines including Yahoo and Alta Vista. It provides a few dozen webpages in response to a search. Some are very interesting. It's particularly good when looking for how to remove mildew from clothing, how to preserve wood shingles, and other questions that may have been studied by a university somewhere. Free downloadable software is installed on your computer and is available at **http://www.copernic.com/index.html**

Section IV Boards, Groups, and E-mail

15

Message Boards and Newsgroups

We were dragged, kicking and screaming, into adding a message board to the El Toro Info Site. Two of our emerging competitors in the growing field of El Toro-related websites started boards, and we feared we might lose market share to them if we didn't provide the same feature.

Still we resisted providing a platform for anonymous antagonists to throw insults at each other's intelligence. There was much of that early in the game. We saw our website in a different light. More than once, I censored a post and told someone to start their own website if they felt they had a right to publish their comments on the World Wide Web. Don't do it on my dime.

There's a great deal to learn about message boards. We've come to see a good side to them. The quality of the posted content has gone up at least as far as El Toro is concerned. The jerks lose interest as the novelty wears off.

None of the pro-airport websites includes a board. They are one-sided in their reporting and would get beat up by viewers if they allowed message boards. Websites that won't include links to sites with opposing views won't tolerate a message board for opposing views.

Pro-airport posters come to the primarily anti-airport boards to pick their fights.

Message boards are like neighborhood bars. The ones that do best are convenient, have congenial hosts, and are frequented by interesting regulars. We will have more to say on the matter in the final chapter of this book.

Technical details of the board do not matter greatly so long as they are user-friendly.

The most convenient, like ours and the popular volunteer-run El Toro Chronicles board require no registration, and anyone can jump on.

OCNow.com, a commercially operated third major El Toro board, requires that everyone register. Forget your sign on ID and you are out of luck. I never go there for that reason.

Our newspapers started moderated websites where every post is reviewed before going onto the board. They have staff to do this. It keeps out dirty words, nasty thoughts, and is about as much fun as a neighborhood bar run by the Temperance Union. These boards received few visitors and some have shut down.

At least one of the volunteer-run boards also folded. There are a limited number of good regular posters, and they don't have time to frequent more than a couple of boards.

El Toro Info Site message board

Our message board software is free of cost from Discusware. Click on a link on our Message Board labeled **Program Credits,** and you will find information to help you install a similar board on your site:

> This discussion forum is an implementation of the Discus discussion board program developed by DiscusWare, LLC of Holland, Michigan. All Discus scripts and static files were authored by Kevin W. Paulisse with design ideas and implementation advice from William F. Polik. Original development of the Discus program was performed at Hope College.

Discus is free and can be downloaded immediately. To learn more about Discus or to download your free copy, visit DiscusWare's web site. **http://www.discusware.com/discus/index.php**

DiscusWare, LLC gratefully acknowledges the following individuals and organizations for their support of the initial development of the Discus program:

Hope College Office of Computing and Information Technology
Hope College Chemistry Faculty
Hope College Chemistry Students
Howard Hughes Medical Foundation Faculty Development Grant
National Science Foundation
Beta Testers

As noted above, the Discus software used on the El Toro Info Site does not require registration. However, it does label each post with the IP address of the posting computer.

The software includes a profanity filter that blocks objectionable words selected by the webmaster. I thought I had a complete vocabulary, but our viewers have come up with a few new ones to convey their feelings about the airport project. Since the poster's IP address is automatically made a part of each message, the filter also can be used to block all messages from any persistently abusive user. Just add their IP address to the dirty word list.

The Discus board enables either users or the website team to create topics or threads to which viewers add. Each topic is automatically assigned a unique URL or address.

This is a useful feature. Frequently there will be a controversial article added to the main **News Section** of the website. We start a new thread on the subject and link to it from the news with "Click here to post your comments."

As discussed earlier, when a San Diego newspaper criticized Orange County voters for rejecting the airport project, we started a message board thread entitled, "San Diego butts in." In a news article summarizing the editorial, we wrote,

El Toro Info Site report, April 27, 2002

San Diego Butts In

In a classic bit of chutzpah, the San Diego Union-Tribune has weighed into the El Toro debate editorially to scold Orange County for not building Southern California's next commercial airport. Orange Countians have never dared to insert themselves into the raging debate over whether San Diego should expand its Lindbergh Field or build elsewhere in that county.

We sense the hand of Orange County pro-airport political operatives, and Mike Gordon's allies from the LAX area, orchestrating yesterday's editorial pronouncement from the San Diego paper, "El Toro Vote Will Harm Southern California".

What do the editorial writers in San Diego know about the deficiencies of El Toro? Have they seen ALPA's pronouncement that it is "an accident waiting to happen"? Have they read the FAA's airspace report about El Toro delaying most flights from John Wayne and Long Beach? Are they aware that the Air Traffic Controllers Union says OCX should lead to the closing of John Wayne? Do they care if our roads are gridlocked and our air fouled?

I think not. Click here to read the article. We've added a link for our well-informed viewers to send a letter to the newspaper's editor and hope that you also will post a copy of what you write on the message thread.

One of the best features of a message board is that users can provide a running collection of the full text of all the relevant news stories, editorials, and letters to the editor from every paper in the region and excerpts from the radio and TV news. In our area there are over three-dozen daily and weekly papers plus the national press that carry airport related stories. On any given day one will find three to eight articles from Orange County papers, surrounding counties, the Sacramento news, Associated Press, the NY Times, Wall Street Journal, and USA Today. If it has a website our viewers seem to find the story. Then they post it.

The day's news is often posted on our site by early rising viewers before I wake up and begin to select the lead articles to be digested and analyzed for our regular **Today's Headlines** page. We refer to these posts as our **Early Bird** thread. The message board becomes a treasure trove of news coverage when you have an enthusiastic group of posters.

Because viewers post the stories, and we do not, we don't run into copyright arguments with the sources.

A useful attribute of this software is that the posts cluster under topics created by the website team or viewers. Threads can be followed for weeks. A representative batch of posts on the message board looks something like this with links to each message:

Typical threads on the El Toro Info Site message board

Early Bird News….Week of May 6, 2002
Media Watcher-05/09, 08:04 am-ONT to reopen parking spaces
Media Watcher-05/09, 08:21 am-Letter writer urges study for an airport
Media Watcher-05/09, 12:57 pm-People around Ontario, March base
Media Watcher-05/09, 01:53 pm-Great Pork Agran's plan for a Great
parrotpaul-05/10, 06:23 am-Anti-El Toro group attacks alternative
parrotpaul-05/10, 06:29 am-Santa Ana district, Tustin end base
parrotpaul-05/10, 07:47 am-Issa wants El Toro provision in defense
ThomasDad-05/10, 10:45 am-But when the redistricting takes place
Gremlin-05/10, 10:57 pm-So Wagner was under Bloomer?
parrotpaul-05/11, 06:19 am-V-plan backers want supervisors
prow-05/11, 08:01 am-For Coad to approve this she would have

Contribution Money…
Taylor-05/10, 10:39 am-What happens to all the contribution
prow-05/10, 11:17 am-Im hoping that the website will
Gremlin-05/10, 12:15 pm-I think that this site should become a
AFinMB-05/10, 06:55 pm-I think we should focus on the wastful
sbayhills-05/11, 08:03 am-I think a little money should be spent
mvmike-05/11, 09:14 am-First, and I hate to be the bearer of
EDITOR-05/11, 10:04 am-This website is not going away until

OCRAA goin'down the tubes—from Len's news page
DBinLF-05/10, 12:37 pm-From my old Marine days, I always
mvmike-05/10, 04:19 pm-I met Art Bloomer just once, for a
Gremlin-05/10, 06:47 pm-I dont know what OCRAAs Mission
sbayhills-05/11, 08:10 am-Any status as a respected commanding

VPLAN.......WHAT V PLAN?

George Leclercq-05/10, 10:19 am-Thanks DBinLF, you pass the reading

ThomasDad-05/10, 10:32 am-And once again, the messenger receives

George Leclercq-05/10, 10:36 am-Dont worry ThomasDad, Im used

ThomasDad-05/10, 10:39 am-How perfect. If you read the V Plan ad

etinotlogical-05/10, 12:54 pm-I like the third ad on their web-site

JERTOMLEHRER-05/10, 01:55 pm-I think that the release of the

AFinMB-05/10, 07:00 pm-And again I ask...how did the New

AOneL-05/11, 12:55 am-AF, following up on your logo comment,

El Toro Chronicles

One of our friendly competitors jumped into the message board arena in May 2000 and won the hearts and minds of activists with a very user-friendly board.

The Chronicles board is an "in" place to post. It provides no content other than a few links and its viewers' posts. Still, it attracts lots of message traffic from a well-informed audience of hard core anti-airport activists. As with the Early Bird thread on the El Toro Info Site, Chronicle's staple is full text newspaper news and viewers' comments on the news. As discussed in several other places in this book, good news content is the key to a high traffic issues-oriented website.

This board and the El Toro Info Site cooperate on the same anti-airport team. Visitors to the Chronicles board frequently copy and post news from our El Toro website since we are often ahead of the newspapers with important stories. Chronicles also includes a prominent link to our website, and viewers move back and forth between the two sites.

I also post information there under my moniker EDITOR, because the Chronicles regulars include an important cadre of volunteer workers in the anti-airport fight. In a high tech version of Gresham's Law, good message board content eventually drives out poor content. Chronicle's content is good.

The moderator Brad McCown, who posts as **JohnQPublic@ occonnect.com**, is a helpful guy who has never hesitated to give me technical advice when needed.

The Chronicles board software is Webb BBS5.0 shareware available for $50. Information on obtaining it is online at **http://awsd.com/ scripts/webbbs/**

The board format has posts wandering down the page with viewers jumping onto the middle or tail end of threads. The dialog does not cluster as conveniently under topics as with the El Toro Info Site board. Instead, each poster puts a header on his or her contribution.

Posts marked "*NT*" include no text other than the header.

The board works because it's fast, easy, and informative, and the users are familiar with the procedure. Note that some of the same posters use this and the El Toro Info Site board above.

Visit the Chronicles board at **http://occonnect.com/eltoro/ etboard.cgi**

Typical threads on the El Toro Chronicles message board

Second Airport Proposal Hits a Downdraft…LA Times…5/28/02 (views: 21)—Sam Adams—5/28/02 06:02

No shocker to us, LA Times! See ya, Russ! *NT* (views: 2)—mikeb—5/28/02 06:24

Re: Second Airport Proposal Hits a Downdraft…LA Times…5/28/02 (views: 11)—sbayhills—5/28/02 06:39

> "others who savaged Orange County's proposed layout" (views: 4)—NY Chief—5/28/02 07:26

> Russell sure knows how to win friends *NT*—Sam Adams—5/28/02 07:30

>> Q&A: [LGB] Airport has a friend in business—LB Press Telegram 5/27/02 (views: 19)—Media Watcher—5/27/02 11:33

>>> Can the feds override the LB of JWA legal agreements? (views: 18)—mvmike—5/27/02 13:28

>>> this article questions federal control constitutionality……..(views: 13)—jabba—5/27/02 18:39

>>> constitutionality issues (views: 5)—mvmike—5/28/02 04:15

Spitzer's style may be cramped—OC Register Buzz 5/27/02 (views: 29)—Media Watcher—5/27/02 11:09

> I wonder if these guys left a cargo door down in san diego……….(views: 30)—jabba—5/27/02 08:45

Airline security is still a myth, even after all the recent security hoopla (views: 14)—mvmike—5/27/02 13:21

We need security like Israeli's airlines..........(views: 10)—jabba—5/27/02 18:28

Check out this healthy exchange from the AWG site (views: 26)—sbayhills—7/13/02 07:33

well I hope they get.........(views: 20)—jabba—7/13/02 09:07

Re: well I hope they get.........(views: 23)—Ernie—7/13/02 10:02

thats right.........(views: 21)—jabba—7/13/02 16:15

OCNow.com El Toro Voices

OCNow.com is a commercial venture—an Internet news outlet that deals with numerous subjects of interest to Orange County residents including local news, movies, weather, traffic, and of course, the El Toro debate. It is funded through the sale of advertising like a print newspaper. The website operates bulletin boards on several topics.

Its El Toro section consists of a small amount of content and a message board. OCNow.com offered the first El Toro message board. However, serious El Toro buffs have moved on to the El Toro Info Site or the Chronicles board. Occasionally we'll see a zealot from one of these two sites posting invitations on OCNow.com trying to recruit viewers to come over to their favorite hangout. It's not good cricket, but it's done.

The board shows only the first post of each thread and the number of responses. Viewers click on the post to read what follows, one post at a time. Navigation is slow. Registration is required.

- El Toro Airport by OC_Av8r, May 27, 02:27...2 Message(s)

- Why in the world by TheHighEnd, May 24, 22:16...6 Message(s)

- Hey Cr8nfun! by ThomasDad, May 22, 13:49...5 Message(s)

- how low can you go??????? by methinks, May 15, 08:26...5 Message(s)

- Message from Russell! by ChrisinLN, May 16, 19:22...2 Message(s)

- STABLE AT THE MARINE BASE by baca53, May 15, 01:58...1 Message(s)

Visit the OCNow.com board, and examine its format more closely, at **http://www.ocnow.com/news/special/eltoro/torovoices.html**

Weblogs

Weblogs or blogs are online journals of sequential posts from one or more individuals. The initiator controls access for posting so that his or her blog tends to focus on a single subject. This differentiates blogs from the wide-open unmoderated message boards discussed above where anyone can post on any thread. Blogs may be publicized for the dissemination of information or used for private communications within an activist group.

A weblog can be added to an existing website. Pyra Lab's Blog*Spot website offers technical advice and free hosting. For more information visit **http://www.blogger.com**.

Newsgroups

Newsgroups are another means for activists to circulate information. Since posts are member-submitted, they have characteristics in common with single-subject message boards. However, newsgroup postings are e-mailed to group members. Typically, newsgroups provide a method for subscribers to restrict delivery of messages to one batch a day.

Aviation Watch e-mail bulletins reach anti-airport activists around the world via a Yahoo newsgroup. Organizing a newsgroup might help your issues-oriented campaign to share information amongst like-minded individuals. See **http://groups.yahoo.com/group/** for details.

16

Building and Operating your E-mail List

An e-mail list is a vital adjunct to the activist's website. E-mail reaches your viewers on those many days when they turn on their computers but don't visit your website. E-mail delivers the specific message you choose for that day from amongst the website's many messages. E-mail can deal with a topic that is hot today while the website deals with matters of continuing interest.

To take advantage of the dynamic qualities of e-mail assign a high priority to building a mailing list.

In this chapter we look at some technical issues related to building and operating an e-mail list. The next chapter will look at how we employ this tool to serve our mission.

When you attend a meeting and publicize the website, it makes good sense to provide a means for attendees to sign up for e-mail.

If you use a signup sheet, it is important that you or another volunteer be there to monitor it. In our experience, roughly one-quarter to one-third of the e-mail addresses people provide in writing are unusable. People write a letter "l" that is indistinguishable from the numeral "1". Some leave a website address instead of their e-mail address. Some misspell, and some write illegibly. Others leave you guessing whether their server address ends with .net or .com by writing "Johnsss@att."

The most useable addresses come via e-mail where they can be copied and pasted into a list without retyping.

We have three principal sources for e-mail addresses in addition to the signup sheets. We use lists from our allied grass roots groups. We collect the largest number of highly motivated individuals through our website. Lastly, we employ the open government laws to obtain addresses of individuals who request El Toro e-mail from governmental sources such as the county.

We never send e-mail to anyone who hasn't requested it and each of our bulk e-mail bulletins includes instructions as to how to unsubscribe from our list. Spam, unsolicited e-mail, is unpopular with recipients and turns people off. Laws in some states regulate spam.

We send our bulletins to approximately 17,000 addresses.

Subscribing on the website

To collect addresses on the website, we include a signup link at the top of our most visited webpage, **Today's Headlines**. It is placed prominently next to a graphic of an envelope with a large script **e**.

SUBSCRIBE FOR SPECIAL NEWS BULLETINS AND ALERTS

Click icon above to receive website e-mail news bulletins. Get information not covered elsewhere. Addresses are kept strictly confidential. We never share our e-mail list!

Clicking on the link takes viewers to this page:

Welcome!!!

TO SUBSCRIBE, CLICK HERE AND THEN SEND

Welcome to the El Toro Info Site's free and strictly private mail list. We never share this list with anyone.

The El Toro Airport website has been in existence since 1996 and the volunteer team has assembled hundreds of pages of information regarding the reuse of MCAS El Toro. The following are amongst the most read pages.

(We then provide the new viewer with a survey of several important website pages and features.)

SPREAD THE WORD. E-mail this message to your list of friends. Please tell your neighbors about the El Toro website at **http://www.eltoroairport.org**

The <u>CLICK HERE</u> link opens a preformatted message block addressed to the website.

To: Editor@eltoroairport.org

Subject: Subscribe to Airport News

Message: Please press the Send button and the El Toro newsletters will be sent to your e-mail address.

Each webpage-editing program includes a method for creating this type of preformatted message. In Netscape, we do it with this statement as a link:

mailto:Editor@ElToroAirport.org?Subject=Subscribe to Airport News&Body=Please press the Send button and the El Toro newsletters will be sent to your e-mail address

The viewer sends the e-mail and we receive it with the sender's address.

We collect the incoming requests in a separate mail folder using a filter on our incoming mailbox set to sort messages with the subject word "Subscribe".

In Netscape filters are created using the Mail Filters option in the drop down Edit menu. In Outlook Express use the Mail Rules option in the drop down Tools menu.

We copy and paste the addresses, separated by commas, into a large Word for Windows text file.

We regularly back up this valuable address file to a floppy disk or CD.

Government lists

We obtain many e-mail addresses from local government. Under California law e-mail lists collected by elected officials and government agencies are records subject to disclosure under the Public Records Act. An earlier chapter discusses how we use such open government laws to our advantage.

Needless to say our pro-airport county officials were surprised when we demanded the e-mail addresses of everyone who had submitted one to the county's El Toro website or who had otherwise signed up for e-mail. These were individuals who requested e-mail about the airport project, and therefore our messages to them did not constitute spam. We are very careful to make it easy for recipients to unsubscribe.

Sending e-mail

We never disclose the names on our list. We use the "blind copy to" or bcc addressing option that exists in most mail software when sending bulk e-mail.

Many e-mail senders unwisely expose every address in their message headers. AOL makes hiding addresses difficult by requiring that bcc's be enclosed in parenthesis. Therefore, users are very apt to reveal their lists, which can be scooped up by professional spammers.

Initially, when our list was a few hundred addresses long, it was easy to send bulk e-mails. We would open our Word file of addresses, highlight all of the addresses, and then copy and paste them into the address line of a message block.

However, when the list grew to several hundred addresses we started to have problems. Messages were not going through to all of the intended recipients. In a runaround typical of the computer world, our Internet Service Provider sent us to our software source, which blamed our ISP and sent us back to them. Eventually we discovered Netscape timed out when the addresses list was too long. We began breaking our list into blocks of about 150 names and sending in several batches.

To keep down the size of the list we collected all our messages that came back as undeliverable in a separate file. This is done with another mail filter. It was time consuming and boring work. Messages occasionally bounce from valid addresses because of temporary problems. Therefore, we wait until an address bounces three times before purging it. John Santora wrote a small program to facilitate the process.

Eventually, sending 150 messages at a time grew too tedious, and we switched to Eudora's mail program. You can acquire Eudora Light as a free download and be able to send larger batches of mail. For this program, visit **http://eudora.qualcomm.com/eudoralight/**

Soon we outgrew Eudora's limit and began breaking the list into batches of a few thousand messages at a time.

Fortunately, a website hosting firm in the community, whose owner shared our feelings about the airport, volunteered to host our outgoing mail service for free as their contribution to the cause. Life became much easier. The professional host not only facilitates sending messages but also provides automatic unsubscribing at the request of the recipient.

Our e-mail host recently found an unexplainable corruption in their files that rendered most of our mailing list, and their most recent backups of the list, unusable. From past experience, I keep a clean backup on my personal computer. There is a message in that.

Management of a large address list can be very time consuming. Adding new names as described above is relatively easy.

Deleting recipients who want to opt out is a bigger challenge. The problem is compounded when an addressee subscribes from one address and then asks to unsubscribe using another. We are expected to be clairvoyant and figure out that **bighotdog@hotmail.com**, who subscribed from home, is the same person as **jgsmithe@ajaxplumbing.com** who now wants to unsubscribe.

Every bulk message we send concludes with this note:

> To be removed from this e-mail list click on **http://www. eltoroairport.org/new_subscribers/A-unsubscribe.html**

PLEASE DO NOT REPLY TO THIS E-MAIL since removal is an automatic process that ONLY can be done from your computer. Thank you.

That still seems to be too difficult for many folks. Some people become abusive when they can't get off a list. Every few months we take a couple of hours and try to clean up the problem cases that collect in a mail box set up with a mail filter to collect the unsubscribe requests.

A final note: If you have the money there are professional mail servers that will do the whole job for you. The El Toro Reuse Planning Authority, a governmental organization that participates in the fight over El Toro, uses Grassroots Enterprises probably the Cadillac of the business. See their offerings at **http://www.grassroots.com/**. If you can afford $50,000 or more for such a professional operation, you probably don't need to spend time reading the remainder of this book.

This chapter dealt with some of the nuts and bolts of building and operating an e-mail list in conjunction with your website. The next chapter discusses what you can do with this important tool.

17

"E-mail Based Democratic Activism"

On March 17, 2002, twelve days after the election that killed the airport project, Stephen Burgard, editorial writer for the Los Angeles Times, observed:

> In the newer suburbs, residents with concerns about quality of life have mobilized and created a new kind of e-mail-based democratic activism centering on the environment and growth. Meanwhile, older neighborhoods have lagged behind in the computer age, threatening to leave the county with its own version of the so-called digital divide.

Had he called it "Internet-based democratic activism," it would have made a great title for this book. As written, it fits this chapter about political use of the e-mail tool.

Why e-mail?

It is essentially free to the activist. No postage is needed.

It quickly reaches a wide audience. Most website viewers do not log on every day to check the news. The majority of the El Toro Info Site viewers visit the website only a few times each month. Consequently, on any given day we can reach almost ten times as many of our followers by e-mail as we can reach by the website itself.

That makes e-mail a very potent tool when something needs to be done. Use e-mail for the most time sensitive purposes.

- To inform, when it is important to get the word out quickly.

- To generate attendance at meetings and rallies.

- To solicit manpower or money.

- To launch e-mail blitzes to government and industry officials.

Getting out the word quickly—with your own spin—is vital to shaping public opinion. When there is important news regarding an issue, you cannot rely on the traditional media to convey your interpretation of its importance to your position.

Television reporting on local issues often is superficial because reporters cover so many different topics. They may not have an indepth appreciation of the subject. Newspaper reporters specialize more, but still, the impact of newspaper coverage sometimes depends more on which person writes the headline than on which one writes the story.

For best results, use e-mail in conjunction with the website. We post analyses and the full text of important documents on the site—with supporting documents such as an FAA report, or a letter from the Air-Line Pilots Association—and include a brief summary with the page link in the e-mail. Our viewers frequently learn the essential elements of the breaking news before the story makes it to the newspapers.

This rapid e-mail response to news means our side of the story reaches supporters, motivates them, spreads to whomever they reach by word of mouth, and provides our activists with a head start on getting letters to the editors published in the papers.

E-mail creates participation

E-mail is an excellent way to generate attendance at meetings. While printed flyers played a role, our focused e-mail helped to produce anti-airport rally crowds of up to 2,000 people.

If individuals concerned with your issue are geographically dispersed, it helps to build a database of e-mail plus snail mail addresses. Some of our addressees are sorted geographically in an Excel spreadsheet. It provides a means to target messages to those who live near an upcoming meeting or rally and to not bother addressees in other areas. We notify residents of important city council meetings and provide speaking tips on crucial issues coming up for discussion or a vote.

Use e-mail to obtain volunteer help. Placing an initiative on the ballot to stop the El Toro airport required the collection of a mass of signatures on petitions. Approximately 2,000 volunteers, reporting to over 30 area captains gathered 175,000 signatures in two months time. Many of the volunteers were recruited by e-mail.

During the signature drive the area captains used e-mail to gather volunteers to man tables set up in front of key markets and at community events. They sent messages like, "Volunteers needed Saturday and Sunday afternoon at the Costco store in Irvine", or "Signature gatherers will be at the San Clemente Ocean Festival next weekend. Call me."

We also created a special bulletin board thread on the website for captains to post their manpower needs. The use of message boards is covered in another chapter.

As Election Day approached, our e-mails focused on the GOTV (Get Out The Vote) effort. Messages reminded viewers to get their new neighbors, and children who recently turned 18, to register to vote.

Viewers were reminded to obtain and submit absentee ballots to insure that they voted. E-mail messages contained instructions on where and how to do this.

We solicited locations for campaign yard signs by bulk e-mail.

E-mail, linked to a website, also is a cost-effective way to raise money. We regularly sent messages with imbedded links to the webpage for our online credit card contributions. Click on the link in the e-mail and you were at the page for donating. The cost compared to snail mail solicitations is negligible. A chapter of this book is devoted to the techniques of doing this.

Our website receives nearly double the number of visitors on weekdays as compared to weekend days. This is opposite to the newspaper pattern where Sundays get the most readers. People use their computers at work to access the Internet and personal e-mail. Therefore, try to get time sensitive messages, especially those tied to website pages, to viewers well before the weekend.

Blitzing

E-mailing to an activist group facilitates their blitzing of government and industry officials. E-mail can include links for immediate access to the target; regular direct mail is not as potent for generating responses. When the County Board of Supervisors is about to vote on a key issue or when a committee in the State Assembly is hearing a bill that concerns us, we may ask our troops to send messages.

You can do this in one of several ways. One method is to build a webpage that fully explains the issue and provides bullet points for writers. The webpage includes an imbedded link to the target individual's e-mail address. Then, bulk e-mail is sent out directing viewers to the page.

This technique is most useful when issues are complex, messages are to go to several individuals on a committee, or where we request a copy of the messages that are sent. Many viewers find it easy to highlight, copy, and paste parts of a webpage into their message.

A California legislative committee reported receiving 800 citizen e-mails on one contentious measure. While they were not all ours, and certainly not all read, they were counted. We played our part by alerting our list and directing them to an informational webpage with links to the committee.

Here is the text of the page we used for the blitz, as a model, or see it with the links at
http://www.eltoroairport.org/involved/sacramento-8-21-00.html.

Sacramento Scheming

In these closing days of the California legislative session, scores of bills are being pushed through in a mad crush of legislation. It is an opportunity for pro-airport lobbyists to sneak amendments into unrelated bills and try to make them law.

We know of several attempts that are being made right now:

- To block Irvine's annexation of the base,

- To prevent the voters from overturning Measure A which zoned El Toro for aviation use,

- To gut Measure F and give the Board of Supervisors sole authority over airport decisions

We need everyone to demand fair treatment from the Legislature.

A bill in the California Assembly, AB1556—having nothing to do with El Toro—has been amended by pro-airport forces to block Irvine's annexation of the base property.

If Irvine annexes the land, county Measure A—which zoned it for airport—would no longer apply.

City zoning could designate the property for non-aviation use, such as a Great Park or mixed park-residential-educational and business use. The voters would decide.

Click on the message block below to send a message to your Orange County State Senators, and the State Senate Committee reviewing the bill on August 25.

1. Insert a Subject such as "AB1556", "Allow Annexation of El Toro", or "Stop undemocratic change in annexation rules"

2. Type a message using some of the following points:

- Vote "No" on any bills that deprive Orange County voters of say over El Toro land use.

- Reject annexation rule changes that remove LAFCO (Local Area Formation) control over El Toro.

- Orange County voters are overwhelmingly opposed to an airport at El Toro. Don't allow the will of the people to be thwarted.

- El Toro reuse is a local, not state issue. Voters passed Measure F so they could decide on the use of the base.

- If Irvine can annex it, the voters are likely to authorize a wonderful park on the land.

- 450,000 Orange County voters passed Measure F by 67.3% because they object to a noisy, polluting airport in the heart of their county. Changing the rules is undemocratic.

3. Append your name and address and send the message.

4. * Click here for pre addressed message form. *

4B. If the above link does not work on your browser, click here for the Committee Chairman

The second link was added to account for the differences between Netscape and Microsoft browsers.

You also can launch blitzes on business leaders who come out with a position on the wrong side of your issue. When the founder of the Carl's Junior restaurant chain sent a letter of support for the airport project to the county—at the urging of a pro-airport business group—we published his letter. We also sent e-mail to our list providing the restaurant's address.

As a result, we received and published the following from the chain:

CKE Restaurants, Inc.

July 10, 1997

It recently was brought to my attention that our Chairman Emeritus, Carl N. Karcher, wrote a letter to the County of Orange, dated October 9, 1996, expressing his support for the proposed Community Reuse Plan for El Toro, which subsequently was published on The El Toro Airport Info Site web page.

Please allow me to clarify that Mr. Karcher's letter represents his personal opinion and does not represent the opinion of CKE Restaurants, Inc. or Carl Karcher Enterprises, operator of Carl's Jr. restaurants. It is my understanding that Mr. Karcher has since written to the County of Orange to clarify that his position on the airport is personal. CKE Restaurants has not taken a position with regard to an international airport in El Toro, and we regret that Mr. Karcher's letter left the impression that his personal opinion was also that of CKE Restaurants, Inc. or Carl's Jr. restaurants.

Sincerely, William P. Foley II
Chairman and CEO
CKE Restaurants, Inc.

A simpler alternate approach is to outline the issue and key points to be made and put the information directly into a bulk e-mailing along with the target individual's address.

The syntax for creating a link to an email address within an e-mail message looks like this:

mailto:editor@eltoroairport.org

The syntax for a link to a webpage from within an e-mail looks like this:

http://www.eltoroairport.org

Unfortunately, AOL users, who are the largest fraction of the potential audience, do not receive either of these as links and could be confused. Many viewers end up returning their message to the sender instead of to the intended addressee.

To place a link in an AOL message, and some CompuServe messages, requires a more complex syntax that will look odd to your non-AOL recipients:

> To write to our editor

> <a href="mailto:editor@eltoroairport.org">CLICK HERE</a>

However, both methods work well enough to enable you to produce an attention getting burst of messages to the target official.

Formatting e-mail bulletins

E-mail needs to be concise. Long messages in narrative form do not receive careful reading. Following the style of the messages sent by major commercial operators like Travelocity and Amazon, we rely on headlines, short statements and judicious use of capitalization.

The subject must stand out and be clear in a long list of messages received by the addressee.

> Subject: **HASTA LA VISTA, EL TORO**

> News summary from the volunteer-run EL TORO INFO SITE

> **http://www.eltoroairport.org**
> 1. Navy makes it final…No aviation for El Toro.
> 2. Chuck Smith reports, "Airport is dead."
> 3. Forget the lawsuits; Save your money.
> 4. Marines' return not covered.
> 5. LAX legislator seeks to penalize O.C.
> 6. To Unsubscribe from these e-mails

> --

1. NAVY ISSUED DECISION TODAY

On March 5, voters killed El Toro airport by a vote of 58 to 42 percent. On April 16, the Board of Supervisors voted to back Irvine's plan for a non-aviation development of the base. On April 23, the Department of Navy issued a Record of Decision (ROD) for non-aviation reuse of the base.

"The Navy has determined that mixed land use is consistent with the Orange County general plan as recently amended by the passage of Measure W…Department of Navy and the General Services Administration (GSA) will consult closely with the El Toro Local Redevelopment Authority and the City of Irvine to determine the appropriate way to dispose of the property, while balancing the needs of the local community and the United States Government."—From the Navy ROD

The Assistant Secretary of the Navy wrote that he "will be taking a team to meet with the City [of Irvine] on April 25th" to discuss the future use of the land.

Full text and analysis of the ROD is available on the El Toro Info Site. See Today's Headlines page for news that updates daily.

http://www.eltoroairport.org

----

2. AIRPORT ADVOCATE SAYS, "WE BETTER START WORKING ON ALTERNATIVE PLANS ".

Supervisor Chuck Smith, the leading airport advocate on the Orange County Board of Supervisors, told the Southern California Regional Airport Authority (SCRAA) Board of Directors meeting last week that the Navy "made it clear that the airport is dead."

"We better start working on alternative plans and not rely on El Toro," he said.

----

3. STOP THE LAWSUITS AND POLITICS AGAINST MEASURE W.

Continued litigation by airport supporters is a waste of money. While it continues, follow the lawsuits at **http://www. eltoroairport.org/news/litigation.html**

A small group of Newport Beach residents and the Orange County Regional Airport Authority (OCRAA) are struggling to try to get another El Toro airport plan onto the ballot.

IT'S TOO LATE...STOP THE WASTE OF TIME AND MONEY.

If you live in one of these OCRAA cities, tell your City Council to save the city's money:

ANAHEIM, BUENA PARK, COSTA MESA, CYPRESS, GARDEN GROVE, LA HABRA, LOS ALAMITOS, NEWPORT BEACH, PLACENTIA, SEAL BEACH, STANTON, VILLA PARK, WESTMINISTER, YORBA LINDA.

It is time for these cities to resign from OCRAA and stop beating the airport dead horse.

----

4. MARINES' RETURN NOT COVERED

The Navy Record of Decision, issued today, makes no mention of retaining land for Marine use.

Two congressional representatives from San Diego are opposed to the Marines moving the Recruit Depot to El Toro from its present location in San Diego.

The move would require an estimated $500 million and an act of Congress.

The Commandant of the Corps has not decided that El Toro is the best place for the Depot. He wants a facility that provides weapons training with live ammunition.

----

5. EL SEGUNDO AND LAX NEIGHBORS IN BID TO PUN-
ISH O.C.

Assemblyman George Nakano, whose district includes LAX, intro-
duced a bill in the State Assembly to penalize Orange County by
withholding highway transportation funds. The bill, AB 2333,
attempts to force expansion of airports other than LAX. It could
impact John Wayne.

Only the City of El Segundo supported it. However, it was
accepted by the Transportation Committee and will move next to
the Appropriations Committee.

Newport Beach and Costa Mesa joined with South County cities
to oppose the bill.

Thank you to the many website viewers who saw the story in our
news and sent e-mails opposing the bill to the State Legislature.

----

6. TO BE REMOVED FROM THIS E-MAIL LIST Click on
**http://www.eltoroairport.org/new_subscribers/A-unsubscribe.
html**

PLEASE DO NOT REPLY TO THIS E-MAIL since removal is
an automatic process. It ONLY can be done from your computer.
Thank you.

It is not an elegant style, but it provides news capsules our viewers
need. We receive many "Thanks for the update" responses. Unless
there is a special need, we try to limit these bulletins to once or at the
most twice a month so as not to over do it

After composing an e-mail bulletin, send it to yourself first and test
all of the links. It is painful to send thousands of messages and then
discover a link does not work because of a typographical error.

18

Raising Money via the Internet

Even grass roots causes need money. The political campaign to pass Measure W and finally defeat the airport at the polls cost approximately $2 million. It all was raised through private contributions from thousands of individual donors.

Online credit card contributions

Roughly five percent of that money came via a credit card link on the El Toro Info Site. That may seem like a small fraction of the total, but it came almost free of cost. Therefore, it represents a significantly larger percent of the total spendable funds netted. Supervisor-elect Chris Norby employed a credit card link on his campaign website and raised a small percentage of his funds that same way.

Other fundraising techniques like regular direct mail solicitations necessitate pouring a substantial part of the gross proceeds into the cost of the mailing lists, design, printing, and postage. It is not unusual for such mailings to just "pay for themselves," meaning that they deliver a message and bring back only enough checks to pay for the mailing. That leaves little or nothing left for other campaign purposes.

Experts at political direct mail working with a good mailing list of previous donors may recover several times the cost. However, activists frequently do not have the financial resources required in advance for a professionally run direct mail campaign.

By contrast, online contributions are essentially "pure profit" to the cause. Up-front costs are nil.

Furthermore, this method taps into sources that may not be on regular mailing lists. Our best results come from e-mail solicitations that include links to the webpage where the credit card form resides. Removing the requirement to get out a checkbook or do much more than click a mouse and type a few lines of data makes the act of contributing instantaneous and simple.

Technical matters

For online credit card contributions, you need a transaction processing organization (TPO) to collect the funds. You will also build a webpage on your site; according to their specifications, with a hyperlink that "jumps" to the TPO's secure website, where the actual financial transaction is performed.

Your website may not support secure communications, so linking to a TPO that does provide this added level of security is a must.

Once the connection is made to the TPO's site, the contributor's name and address and credit card information is transmitted from his or her browser in an encrypted form. The TPO will validate the credit card number and return a "success" or "declined" indication to the contributor. In addition, they keep a detailed history of the transaction on their website.

This is a necessity since your website never sees the credit card or name and address information of the contributor. That information is confidential. You will need to make arrangements with the TPO to have this information, minus the credit card number, collected and sent to your organization if you want to build a list of these financial supporters for later use.

As a paying client of the TPO you have a right to access this information and obtain detailed and summary reports. Your treasurer can access these reports, download the information if necessary, and use this history to reconcile your bank deposits by employing a secure User ID and password.

It is important to check that the link you install is accessible to users of Internet Explorer, Netscape, and AOL. It is frustrating to lose contributions because some popular browsers do not work with the link.

Of secondary importance is the range of credit cards that is accepted. The El Toro Info Site has received a few complaints because its contribution link does not accept American Express or Discover cards.

The El Toro Info Site uses CardService International, a national firm. Their transaction processing service is called LinkPoint. The corporation's website with information about services is at **http:// www.onlinecsi.com/**

The company provides this informative overview of an online credit card transaction:

Step 1

When a consumer decides to buy a product or service online, using common browsers such as Internet Explorer or Netscape Navigator, the secure order form of the merchant prompts the consumer to enter their name, address, ship-to, credit card information, and any other pertinent information required to process the sale.

Step 2

Upon completion of the order form by the consumer, the "Submit" or "Pay Now" button is clicked to begin the payment process.

Step 3

The button is linked to the LinkPoint Secure Payment Gateway which routes and obtains the credit card authorization or declination code. The credit card is checked against the address verification system (AVS) to authenticate the cardholder.

An authorization reduces the available credit limit, but does not actually place a charge on the statement of the cardholder or move money to the merchant.

In line with bankcard association rules, the merchant is not allowed to settle transactions until the ordered goods can be shipped, therefore a time lag may exist between the authorization and the settlement process.

CardService International electronically deposits the money into the checking account of the merchant within 48 hours of settlement.

The Linkpoint help desk and other merchant services are accessible by phone at 1-800-456-5989.

Supervisor-elect Chris Norby's campaign website **http://www.norby2002.com** uses Authorize.net for its TPO. Norby's site nicely integrates the credit card link with information on sending checks by mail. A mail contribution form is available for download as an Acrobat file.

For more on Authorize.net's WebLink services see **http://www.authorize.net/** or call Sales at 1-866-437-0476. The company's website provides this descriptive information.

WebLink works in one of two ways: It either captures the necessary customer information (name, credit card number, etc.) from a merchant's own secure transaction page, or it displays a customizable transaction page hosted on an Authorize.Net secure server, for the customer to fill out.

For non-profits only

One of the anti-airport entities, The Foundation for the Great Park, has Internal Revenue Service non-profit status. Their website routes contributions through eGrants.org, an organization that collects the funds and distributes them to the participating non-profit groups. If you qualify for this tax deductible status contact eGrants:

www.eGrants.org
P.O. Box 29256

San Francisco, CA 94129-0256
(415) 561-7807

The following information from the eGrants.org website is generally true of all card services and may be helpful to bring to the attention of viewers.

Security

eGrants wants you to have complete confidence when you make a donation online; in fact, it's statistically safer to use your credit card over the Internet than in a restaurant or department store. That's because we use Secure Sockets Layer (SSL) technology to encrypt the data that you provide. This allows sensitive information such as your credit card number to be almost unreadable to anyone who wrongly intercepts the information. SSL is supported by all major browsers including Microsoft Internet Explorer (v2.1 or higher) and Netscape Navigator (v2.0 or higher).

More on security

We receive a number of inquiries from would-be contributors who react negatively to not seeing a padlock icon on the lower left of their screen. Our webmaster wrote this technical response that we save and send by e-mail to concerned viewers. Having a message like this one ready may serve you well.

You have requested an explanation as to why you don't see the https on the contribution form or the El Toro site.

1. We are using a 3rd party service to handle all the behind the scenes transaction processing because we have limited resources to do all this processing in-house. The customized transaction page you see initially "comes from" our non-secure server.

2. Then you fill the form out, and the destination address for that outbound transaction does use https. So the data leaves your PC encrypted.

3. Finally, the 3rd party agent receives your encrypted transaction, checks the account information, and sends you a reply. This reply is the tail end of the secure transaction and so you get to see the https in the URL for the first time.

4. When you return to the El Toro site, to a non-contribution page, you'll see the URLs change back to http.

Now to test this for yourself, on this or any other site, you can do the following under Internet Explorer (Netscape has similar settings)

1. From Internet Explorer go to Tools menu, then Internet options, then the Advanced tab.

2. Scroll down to the bottom, under Security.

3. Towards the bottom of the list, you'll see

4. "Warn if changing between secure and not secure mode." Check that option.

5. Now go to the contribution page on the El Toro website and enter a phony credit card number on the page. Click Submit.

The browser should tell you that you are about to go to secure site. Click the "More info" tab on that warning dialog and it will describe in more detail the encryption business.

Again, for places like Amazon, Wells Fargo, and Schwab they send out the first page of the secure part of a transaction because it might contain your account number. If the form they are sending you is blank, there is really no need to encrypt it.

The encryption only needs to start when sensitive data is going down a wire, and that encryption process can be initiated by either side—the website or the PC.

Hope this helps. Let me know if you have any more questions.

Regards, John Santora

The explanation is too technical for some folks, but they find John's obvious command of the matter to be reassuring.

The successful activist on the Internet needs to combine a mix of technical savvy with public relations and political skills to make the process work.

Section V Lessons Learned

19

Evaluating Website Strengths and Weaknesses and Lessons Learned

Winners and losers

Once the El Toro Info Site pioneered Internet coverage of the airport debate others followed. Some created a successful niche in cyberspace, but most did not. This final chapter evaluates the winners and losers in the fight over El Toro-related market share on the web. Analyzing what worked and what did not work for the activists and organizations involved hopefully will help you in your efforts.

Measuring website viewership

What can be achieved quantitatively with an activist website depends, in part, upon the size of its viewership. In attempting to estimate the audience size for each of the El Toro issue websites, and all of the sites combined, it is apparent there is no one standard unit of measurement.

Our team always looked at our **hits**. Hits are a measure provided to us by the web statistics source included as a package with our hosting service. In simple terms hits occur when a viewer requests a page on the site. The page may include numerous elements such as links or graphics. Each element counts as a hit. In a typical visit to the El Toro Info Site a viewer will generate about eight hits. The trend in the number of

169

hits indicates how traffic grows from month to month and how traffic is spread amongst the pages on the site. Not all websites receive data on hits.

Some get **page request or page view** data from their hosts. Visit three pages during a session and this is recorded as three views or requests. This statistic does not provide a good comparison between sites of different kinds. A website with a message board will record many more page requests, because a visitor reading ten posts on the board will be recorded as requesting ten page views.

Another statistic is the number of **visits, visitors, or users**. We receive data on total visits and unique visitors. In the first, you count twice in the total if you go to the website twice. In the second, you count just once for that day. Unfortunately, that is a simplification since the software must determine if you are you when you return for subsequent visits.

On our site, there are two to three hits for each page view and about three page views per visit.

The daily average number of unique visitors, or users, is the most useful statistic for comparing website audiences. However, it does not reveal the number of unique visitors in a month. Are a thousand viewers each returning every day for a month equivalent to thirty thousand different viewers each visiting the site once in a month?

To make matters difficult for anyone trying to gage the total volume of El Toro website traffic, some of the smaller websites do not collect any data.

Finally, none of the pro-airport website operators provided answers to our questions about their viewership.

For a more in-depth understanding of the problems of viewership measurement see WebTrends' page on **Understanding Hits, Page Views and User Sessions**. It is found at **http://www.webtrends.com/ support/hits_views_sessions.htm**

WebTrends, a major provider of usage data, supplies a detailed review of the methods for counting user sessions on their site. This small excerpt is instructive:

> The three most common measurements of web site activity are hits, page views, and user sessions. Following is a description of each.
>
> A hit is a request to a server for a file. Total Hits is the total number of files requested from the server. This number includes all graphics, audio/video files, and other supporting files, as well as the actual HTML page itself. Total Hits includes all requests in the count, whether or not the files were successfully retrieved. Total Successful Hits, on the other hand, refers only to those files that were successfully served.
>
> Page Views (or Page Impressions) is the number of pages viewed, not including the supporting graphic files. Pages are files with extensions such as .htm, .html, .asp (and a few others). By definition, then, the number of total hits is almost always greater than the number of page views. For instance, if a site has one web page with five graphics on it, every time a user visited that page, it would be reported that six hits and one page view or impression occurred.
>
> User Sessions is a measure of the number of unique users who visited a web site during a certain time period. Measuring user sessions is more complicated than measuring hits or page views. The user session statistic can be seen as equivalent to "Unique Visits," which, unless every visitor only sees one page, will be less than the number of page views/impressions.

El Toro website users

This chapter includes best estimates of the viewership volume for the various El Toro websites. A combination of factors were used including quantitative data freely provided by several website operators, informed assumptions as to the relationship of one measurement method to another, and just plain educated opinions from some participants about the others. The sites in this analysis fall into four rough categories of viewership volume and will be so described in the pages that follow:

- Large viewership—1,000 or more average daily visitors or users
- Medium—250 approximate daily visitors
- Small—100 approximate daily visitors
- Miniscule—25 or fewer daily visitors

The El Toro Info Site is the only one to fall well into the large viewership category. Our one site probably has more viewers than all of the others combined.

Some individuals actively concerned with El Toro visit several of the sites when they log on. Hence, the total market size is less than the sum of all of the individual websites because of this duplication.

All of the sites together are estimated to reach an average of fewer than 3,000 unique visitors a day. The number of different visitors over a month's time is estimated to be about ten times that number. We often ask ourselves what that amount of viewership means in terms of market penetration.

How should we feel about 30,000 viewers for the hottest political issue in a county with a population of almost 3 million residents? If that estimate discourages anyone because they have visions of reaching huge numbers of viewers, consider this:

Orange County's 3 million adults and children reside in more than a million households of different configurations. However, only 450,000 -700,000 of these households are classified as showing a "high propensity to vote". Political consultants use differing formulas for defining who is likely to vote.

Probably one-quarter or more of the voting households—say 150-200,000—have computers, but many of these computers are used primarily for e-mail and not for website browsing.

Roughly three-quarters of the county's population lives in cities remote from John Wayne Airport or El Toro. They perceive the airport issue as not touching their personal lives.

Most people who surf the web go to auctions, price travel arrangements, do school projects, read general news, follow their finances, or view pornography. Only a small fraction is interested in websites on political issues.

It is no small achievement to induce 3,000 people (or households) each day, or an estimated ten times that number of different people over the course of a month, to visit a local political website. It has taken several years to build that audience during a period when the overall use of the Internet has exploded.

The good news, as this book states repeatedly, is that the Internet political audience represents an informed and active cadre that spreads the word to the much larger general population.

The El Toro website winners and losers

Readers are encouraged to explore those of the websites that are still online and take note of their attributes. What works and does not work in the airport debate should be instructive for activists employing the Internet in other issues.

Estimates on size of viewership and assessment of each site's strengths and weaknesses are the best I can provide. It is unfortunate that some website operators were unwilling to participate in our survey. This analysis is no attempt to demean the efforts of those that worked on or funded the sites. It is to help others who are not involved with El Toro to gain a sense of what realistically can and cannot be achieved—and through what methods.

1. El Toro Info Site (Large viewership)
http://www.eltoroairport.org

Volunteer run anti-airport website

Strengths:

- Volunteer team provides daily updates.

- Posts news stories that never reach the traditional media or before they get into print. Almost half of news is from the website's own coverage.

- Extensive online library of information.

- "Official" website of the grass roots anti-airport movement.

- Large audience and e-mail bulletins enable the site to generate viewer involvement.

- Hyperlinks to websites on both sides of the debate, newspapers, and elected officials.

- Provides balanced coverage though with an admitted preponderance of anti-airport information. Maintains credibility with media and elected officials.

- Message board is readily organized by topics. One thread carries full text of print media articles. Website news section often includes links to board threads and posts.

Weaknesses:

- Difficult website to maintain because every news posting is edited. Requires seven-day-week coverage by the volunteer web team.

- Homepage does not follow usual layout guidelines with tabs across the top and left side. Relies on **Table of Contents** and built in search engine.

2. El Toro Chronicles (Medium)
http://occonnect.com/eltoro/etboard.cgi

Volunteer run anti-airport bulletin board

Strengths:

- Easy to use message board does not require registration.

- Users are able to edit their messages after they are posted.

- A loyal following of key activists. Many are on the board daily.

- Active viewers post almost every relevant newspaper article on the subject making it an outstanding portal to the press and online news sources.

- A site to be checked more than once a day to make certain not to miss anything.

- Good tool for getting urgent information to a cadre of active citizens.

- Searchable board is useful for finding back articles.

- Convenient links to other relevant websites.

- Maintained by one moderator with viewers providing most of the content.

Weaknesses:

- No content other than that which viewers post.

• Lack of a general news page to draw non-posting viewers.

3. OCNow.com El Toro Voices (Medium)
http://www.ocnow.com/news/special/eltoro/index.html

El Toro section of a non-partisan commercial website

Strengths:

• Some limited content though the El Toro section consists primarily of a bulletin board.

• Website is a commercial operation affiliated with the local cable television and Internet access company. Advertises and draws viewers by covering numerous subjects of local interest besides El Toro. Other pages cover news, weather, sports, movies, etc.

• Professional staff to maintain the pages.

Weaknesses:

• Bulletin board requires registration. Does not seem to draw the "in crowd" of activists.

• Message board is slow and threads ramble all over the subject.

• Pages include popup and banner ads.

4. County of Orange "Just the Facts" website (Medium)

This county funded pro-airport website was taken offline by a court order against spending public funds to influence the outcome of the Measure W election. The El Toro Info Site acquired the address and links it to its homepage.

Strengths:

- Funded as part of a multi-million dollar campaign by the county government to try to sell the airport plan. Major funding enabled this website to provide professional design, extensive information, and attractive graphics. An elaborate simulator provided viewers with information on aircraft noise and flight paths.

- The website cost nearly $150,000 to create and $50,000 to operate for the less than one year it was online.

- Contained useful data not readily available elsewhere.

- Link for building an e-mail list.

Weaknesses:

- Published half of the story. This government-controlled site was strictly pro-airport, avoided open discussion of airport drawbacks, and thereby lost credibility. The "Just the Facts" title became the butt of numerous jokes.

- Not enough new content added to draw viewers back regularly.

- Probably very high cost per visit. The number of visitors was never disclosed.

5. Airport Working Group's Eltoronow.org (Small)
http://www.eltoronow.org/

Pro-airport website. No information available on funding or operations.

Strengths:

- Simple layout and organization of content copied after the El Toro Info Site.

- Easy to operate and maintain. A good format for activists with limited time and funds.

- Posts full text of newspaper articles with editorial comment limited to brief statements added to the headlines.

- Openly advocates the pro-airport position of the Airport Working Group. Makes no attempt to appear bipartisan.

- Links to newspapers and to pro-airport websites.

- Collects e-mail addresses for political use.

- Credit card link.

Weaknesses:

- Hostile one-sided coverage is a potential viewer turnoff. Frequently derides anti-airport cities and their elected officials on issues unrelated to the airport debate.

- Posts crude abrasive cartoons, e.g. depicting anti-airport leaders in Taliban costumes.

- Links are restricted to pro-airport websites and information.

- Prints only pro-airport letters.

- No message board or other means for posting contrary opinions.

- Many viewers are anti-airport activists just checking up on this site's spin rather than the pro-airport sympathizers that it is intended to reach.

- Site does not identify those who are responsible for editorial and cartoon content.

6. El Toro Reuse Planning Authority (Small)

This Joint Powers Authority anti-airport website was taken offline voluntarily following a court order against spending public funds to influence the outcome of the Measure W election.

Strengths:

• Professionally developed website operated for a group of ten anti-airport cities.

• Published the text and graphics of anti-airport direct mail pieces.

• Obtained many of its visitors by purchasing the address **www.eltoroairport.com** when it became available thereby getting viewers who were looking for **www.eltoroairport.org**

• Viewership encouraged by a very expensive but effective e-mail program and direct mail.

Weaknesses:

• Static. Very little changing content to draw visitors a second time.

• Very high cost per visitor. Taxpayer-funded.

7. No on Measure W California Park Tax Assessment Guide (Small-Miniscule)
http://www.ocgreatpark.org/

Political campaign funded pro-airport website

Strengths:

• Clever political tactic created by the Airport Working Group for use during the Measure W campaign. Part of an intense campaign to portray defeat of the airport as resulting in a "Great Tax". The overall campaign message was effective in swaying votes since marginally informed residents normally opt against taxes—though the impact of the website cannot be determined.

- Included a property tax calculator.

- Address of this website was included in the pro-airport arguments printed in the official county Voters Pamphlet and in direct mail.

Weaknesses:

- Contains misleading information from consultants hired for the purpose.

- Directly contradicts county analysis of Measure W.

- Site does not identify the individuals responsible for content.

8. OCX El Toro (Miniscule)
http://ocxeltoro.com/

Volunteer run pro-airport website promoting an alternative to the county's plan

Strengths:

- Lots of nice graphics.

- Main source of information about an alternative airport plan devised by this volunteer group.

- Includes a downloadable petition form and instructions.

- Link for subscribing to e-mail list.

- Identifies the website principals.

Weaknesses:

- Spelling errors and misstatements such as saying contributions are tax deductible when they are not make the site appear amateurish despite the nice graphics. Downloadable petition form does not meet state legal requirements as to content.

- Difficult site to navigate. Some links don't work. Some pages do not load in Netscape.

- The alternative plan presented by this site generated very little interest.

- The volunteer who designed and operated this website gave up the project because of the lack of public interest.

- Mostly visited by anti-airport activists checking on the opposition.

9. Foundation for the Great Park (Miniscule)
http://www.orangecountygreatpark.org/

Professionally developed website for an anti-airport, pro-park fundraising group

Strengths:

- Very attractive and worth a visit.

- Website address included in the group's print mailings is main source of viewers.

- Link for credit card contributions and with gifts for donors.

Weaknesses:

- A static site with nothing much to draw visitors a second time.

- No message board.

- Example of how money can be spent for relatively little benefit. Very high cost per visitor.

10. The Keep John Wayne Airport Working Group (Miniscule) http://www.keepjwaworking.org/

Volunteer created anti-airport webpage poking fun at the Airport Working Group.

Strengths:

- Low cost and effort.

- Contains a few links to other websites and pages.

Weaknesses:

- Static. Hasn't been changed in a year. No reason to go back.

11. The Open Water Plan (Miniscule) http://occonnect.com/trustme/index1.html

Another volunteer created anti-airport website poking fun at Newport Beach

Strengths:

- Low cost and effort.

- Clever and fun. More pages than the site above.

Weaknesses:

- New content is added occasionally. Relatively little reason for going back.

12. John Wayne Airport Limits (Miniscule) http://www.jwalimits.org/

Professionally developed, taxpayer-funded website for the City of Newport Beach

Strengths:

• Simple and well-organized presentation of information on one aspect of the airport debate.

Weaknesses:

• Static. Very little reason to go back a second time.

• Heavy reliance of files that open with Acrobat.

• Probable high cost per visit.

13. OCNow.com Community Links (Miniscule) http://communitylink.ocnow.com

A collection of free webpages offered by OCNow to local clubs and organizations
Due to host's software changes, the El Toro page is no longer on line.

Strengths:

• El Toro Info Site obtained a free page and used it to post occasional news updates. Included a hyperlink to the Info Site's main website that drew a few new viewers.

Weaknesses:

• Hardly anyone knew it existed or visited the page.

• A nuisance to try to remember the host's unique procedures for updating the page.

• Allowed to fall out of date.

14. Millennium Plan.com

This volunteer run website is no longer online

Strengths:

- Two well-known residents of the City of Irvine created this website, which received publicity through city officials and the local newspaper.

- Offered attractive graphics, varied content, and a message board.

- Provided information on potential commercial users of the El Toro property.

- Good presentation of information not available elsewhere.

Weaknesses:

- Competed for market share with the already established El Toro Info Site. After a few months of growth in viewership, the traffic began to slip.

- Message board had technical problems and posts became sporadic.

- Devoted to a commercial reuse plan for El Toro, the "Millennium Plan", which ultimately was abandoned in favor of a park/educational use.

- The website traffic did not justify the significant effort required to keep content current. The site was taken offline.

15. Safe and Healthy Communities
Archived at http://www.eltoroairport.org/safe-and-healthy/

This volunteer run website was created for the 2000 Measure F campaign. It operated in conjunction with the El Toro Info Site. It is inactive.

Strengths:

- Offered an attractive site filled with content provided by the El Toro Info Site team. Contained press releases, endorsement statements, questions and answers, and ballot information regarding the 2000 Measure F campaign.

- Q&A page was a useful handout during the campaign.

- Was advertised in Measure F campaign literature and publicized during television news programs.

Weaknesses:

- Few residents bothered to visit the site. It fell in the Small-Miniscule category of viewership. A regrettable example of a good website that could not generate much of an audience.

- The volunteer who designed and operated the site gave up the project because of the lack of community interest.

Lessons learned

The activist embarking on an Internet campaign must have realistic expectations about the size of the audience that can be reached.

Estimate your cost in money and effort per visitor and decide if it is worth it. Otherwise, you may overreach, lose interest, and your website may become stale and useless.

Work as hard at publicizing your website as you do operating it. Otherwise, no one will know it is there.

Even though the number of website visitors may be modest, the website should provide content that helps these individuals to reach out to the larger offline audience. The website can have major impact beyond the Internet. E-mail links to the newspapers and to elected officials are most useful.

Build an e-mail list. This will enable you to quickly reach a cadre of opinion leaders who can influence others.

Offer a message board and encourage the posting of real news from the mainstream media. If handled right it will attract serious activists and build an informed following. If you don't have the time to write your own daily news coverage, viewer-posted message board news is a good substitute. Consider writing a weekly news summary as an alternative.

Collect selections of content that will further the cause. Build an online library about your issue.

Maintain credibility. Do not become overly partisan.

The outcome of an election frequently can turn on just a few percentage points. The outcome of a council vote may turn on one person. You and the information you provide can make a difference.

Good luck.

Epilogue

During all the years spent fighting the Internet war over El Toro and the months spent writing this book, I knew intuitively that we were not the first, nor the only, nor the best employers of this new tool.

We were too busy fighting battles and putting out fires to seek help. We kept our noses to the grindstone and did little to search beyond the airport-related websites that we knew for other practitioners of Internet activism. Learning more about all of the Internet's capabilities took a back seat to using it on a daily basis.

It was only at the conclusion of my writing of this book that I discovered a resource that would have helped in these efforts. It was on the Internet.

The Virtual Activist 2.0 is an online training course from NetAction; a national nonprofit organization "dedicated to promoting use of the Internet for effective grassroots citizen action campaigns". The course is accessed at **http://www.netaction.org/training/**

Virtual Activist 2.0 and this book overlap on some topics and complement each other in many important ways. Both are useful because no matter how far you go with this subject, there is much to learn.

NetAction takes no position on the airport debate nor do we take any position on the politics of NetAction and its affiliates. We mention it here for the information of our readers.

Afterword

On March 5, 2002 voters passed Measure W eliminating aviation use of El Toro from the Orange County General Plan. However, uncertainty still clouds the fate of the property as this is being written.

A group of airport supporters attempted to qualify a new aviation initiative for the November 2002 ballot. They lacked support and gave up. The Orange County public is not interested in another airport.

The City of Newport Beach and the County Board of Supervisors agreed in June on a proposal for modest expansion of the existing John Wayne airport.

Airport proponents filed a lawsuit in state court seeking to overturn Measure W and to enjoin its implementation. The litigants include some of the same players from Newport Beach who began the airport push in 1994. Airport opponents are confident that their initiative will withstand the legal challenge.

The pro-airport groups also filed a federal lawsuit attempting to block the Department of the Navy from disposing of the base for non-aviation uses. The Navy appears undeterred and intent on selling the land in 2003.

The battle moved to the state capitol in Sacramento and to Washington where pro-El Toro lobbyists are trying to override the will of the voters. Political leaders from communities surrounding Los Angeles International Airport call for "environmental justice" and a "fair share" allocation of future airport capacity to Orange County whether this county wants it or not.

Nothing is predictable in this political context. The endgame that is in our grasp today may not be the final outcome, but only a pause between rounds in the fight over El Toro.

In any case, the Internet skills that we acquired are here for you to use, and if necessary, for us to employ once more.

Glossary of Technical Terms

Browser—A software program that enables the scanning of the World Wide Web. Different browsers have different capabilities and limitations. Popular browsers are Microsoft's Internet Explorer and Netscape's Navigator.

Domain name—The identification of a website on the Internet. The domain for the El Toro Info Site is **www.eltoroairport.org**. Domain names are registered so they are issued to only one owner. Each has a unique numerical IP address. A variety of domain name endings classify the site as .org for non-profit organizations, .com for commercial sites, and .gov for governmental agencies. Domains may be subdivided into numerous pages or URL's.

Emoticon—A symbol or "emotion icon" typed into an e-mail to express a feeling. Emoticons sometimes must be viewed sideways as with "said with a smile" :-D.

FTP—The acronym for File Transfer Protocol. This is the formal set of rules that allows computers to transfer files. For example, FTP software is employed when transferring webpage updates from a personal computer to a website host.

Host—A large computer or server on which a website physically resides and from which pages are forwarded over the Internet upon a viewer's request.

HTML—The acronym for Hypertext Markup Language. A language consisting of letters and characters used for creating documents like those on the Internet's World Wide Web. Popular website editing software programs automatically translate documents into HTML without the user needing to know the language.

Internet—The global network that connects computers and enables them to send text documents including e-mail. See also World Wide Web.

IP address—The unique address for a location on a network. Each website (Web site) has an IP address associated with its host computer. Each viewer's computer has one assigned by the user's ISP. The format of an IP address is a numeric address written as four numbers separated by periods. For example, 68.5.170.86

ISP—Internet Service Provider. A service that connects a computer to the Internet, usually for a fee or in exchange for advertising space. Popular ISPs are AOL, Earthlink, and CompuServe. Some connect by telephone, some by high-speed cable and some by either one.

JPEG or JPG—Two acronyms for Joint Photographic Experts Group. An image compression algorithm that reduces the size of photographic and other image files used in webpages. GIF, Graphics Interchange Format image files also are commonly used on web pages. Images taken with digital cameras must be converted to one of these formats.

Link, hypertext link, or hyperlink—A connection from an-email message or webpage to another webpage created by the use of HTML. The link typically appears in blue and may be underlined. Clicking on the link with the mouse takes the viewer to the target webpage.

OCR—Optical Character Recognition. Software employed with a scanner to produce a text document rather than a graphical representation (picture) of a page of text. The OCR software recognizes each character and word by its shape and converts it into a form that can be manipulated in a word processing program.

URL—The acronym for Universal Resource Locator. The address that identifies a specific resource or page on the Internet. The URL for the El Toro Info Site's March 6, 2002 news story reporting the Measure W election results is **http://www.eltoroairport.org/news/news-0302.html#0306-election**

World Wide Web—The Internet and the Web are separate but related. The Internet is a networking infrastructure in which any computer can communicate with any other computer as long as they are both connected. The World Wide Web, or simply Web, is built on top of the Internet for sharing specially formatted documents. These documents (Web pages or webpages) formulated in HTML may contain graphics, audio, and video files.

24/7—The number of hours per day and days per week that an activist can work.

0-595-23857-2

www.ingramcontent.com/pod-product-compliance
Lightning Source LLC
Chambersburg PA
CBHW061404280526
45784CB00001B/364